D1830659

THE BHAGAVAD GITA

OR

THE LORD'S SONG

Owing to the antiquity and rarity of this book, certain pages are regrettably absent, and readability is compromised due to the blurring of the original text. If you possess any insights regarding the availability of these missing sections, kindly inform us. Your assistance is crucial in ensuring the completion of this significant work for the benefit of future generations.

THE BHAGAVAD GITA

OR

THE LORD'S SONG

TRANSLATED BY

ANNIE BESANT

GYAN

Published by

Gyan Publishing House
5, Ansari Road
Daryaganj, New Delhi-110002
Phone: 011-47034999, 9811692060
E-mail: books@gyanbooks.com

Distribution Network
gyanbooks.com
India, USA, Canada, UK, Australia

© Publisher

All rights reserved. No part of this work may be reproduced, stored, adapted, or transmitted in any form or by any means, electronic, mechanical, photocopying, micro-filming, recording or otherwise, or translated in any language, without the prior written permission of the copyright owner and the publisher.

ISBN: 978-93-6780-114-7 (PB)

First Published, 1895

2nd Impression 2024

Printed at: Gyan Press, Delhi.

The book is sold subject to the condition that it shall not, by way of trade or otherwise, be lent, resold, hired out, or otherwise circulated without the prior publisher's written consent.

THE BHAGAVAD GITA OR THE LORD'S SONG
Author: ANNIE BESANT

THE BHAGAVAD GÎTÂ

OR

THE LORD'S SONG

TRANSLATED BY

ANNIE BESANT

New and Revised Edition

LONDON
THEOSOPHICAL PUBL SHING SOCIETY
26 Charing Cross S. W
NEW YORK: THEOSOPHICAL PUBLISHING SOCIETY
65 Fifth Avenue
BENARES: THEOSOPHICAL PUBLISHING SOCIETY
1896

DEDICATED

TO ALL

ASPIRANTS IN EAST AND WEST

PREFACE.

Among the priceless teachings that may be found in the great Hindu poem of the *Mahâbhârata*, there is none so rare and precious as this, "The Lord's Song." Since it fell from the divine lips of Shrî Krishna on the field of battle, and stilled the surging emotions of his disciple and friend, how many troubled hearts has it quieted and strengthened, how many weary souls has it led to him! It is meant to lift the aspirant from the lower levels of renunciation where objects are renounced to the loftier heights where desires are dead, and where the Yogî dwells in calm and ceaseless contemplation, while his body and mind are actively employed in discharging the duties that fall to his lot in life. That the spiritual man need not be a recluse, that union with the divine Life may be achieved and maintained in the midst of worldly affairs, that the obstacles to that union lie not outside us but within us—such is the central lesson of the BHAGAVAD GÎTÂ.

It is a scripture of Yoga: now Yoga is literally union, and its means harmony with the divine Law, the becoming one with the divine Life, by the subdual of all outward-going energies. To reach this, balance must be gained, equilibrium, so that the self, joined to the Self, shall not be affected by pleasure or pain, desire or aversion, or any of the "pairs of opposites" between which untrained selves swing backwards and forwards. Moderation is therefore the key-note of the GÎTÂ, and the harmonising of all the constituents of man, till they vibrate in perfect attunement with the One, the supreme Self. This is the aim the disciple is to set before him. He must learn not to be attracted by the attractive, nor repelled by the repellent, but must see both as manifestations of the one Lord, so that they may be lessons for his guidance, not fetters for his bondage. In the midst of turmoil he must rest in the Lord of Peace, discharging every duty to the fullest, not because he seeks the results of his actions, but because it is his duty to perform them. His heart is an altar, love to his Lord the flame burning upon it; all his acts, physical and mental, are sacrifices offered on the altar; and once offered, he has with them no further concern.

As though to make the lesson more impressive, it was given on a field of battle. Arjuna, the warrior-prince, was to vindicate his brother's title, to destroy a usurper who was oppressing the land; it was his duty as prince, as warrior, to fight for the deliverance of his nation and to restore order and peace. To make the contest more bitter, loved comrades and friends stood on both sides, wringing his heart with personal anguish, and making a conflict of duties as well as physical strife. Could he slay those to whom he owed love and duty, and trample on ties of kindred? To break family ties was a sin; to leave the people in cruel bondage was a sin; where was the right way? Justice must be done, else law would be disregarded; but how slay without sin? The answer is the burden of the book: Have no personal interest in the event; carry out the duty imposed by the position in life; realise that Îshvara, at once Lord and Law, is the doer, working out the mighty evolution that ends in bliss and peace; be identified with him by devotion, and then perform duty as duty, fighting without passion or desire, without anger or hatred; thus activity forges no bonds, Yoga is accomplished, and the soul is free.

Such is the obvious teaching of this sacred book. But as all the acts of an Avatâra are symbolical, we may pass from the outer to the inner planes, and see in the field of Kurukshetra the battlefield of the Soul, and in the sons of Dhritarâshtra enemies it meets in its progress; Arjuna becomes the type of the struggling soul of the disciple, and Shrî Krishna is the Logos of the soul. Thus the teaching of the ancient battlefield gives guidance in all later days, and trains the aspiring soul in treading the steep and thorny path that leads to peace. To all such souls in East and West come these divine lessons, for the path is one, though it has many names, and all souls seek the same goal, though they may not realise their unity.

In order to gain something of the precision of the Sanskrit, a few technical but fairly familiar terms have been given in the original; Manas is thus retained, and may be explained for non-Theosophical readers as meaning mind, both in the lower mental processes in which it is swayed by the senses, by passions and emotions, and in the higher processes of reasoning; Buddhi is the faculty above the ratiocinating mind, and is the Pure Reason, exercising the discriminative faculty of intuition, of spiritual discernment; if these words are translated in various ways in different passages, as heart, mind, understanding, etc., etc., the Bhagavad Gîtâ loses much of its practical value as a treatise on Yoga, and the would-be learner becomes confused. The adjectival ending "ic" is used in forming adjectives from Sanskrit nouns, although its use is sometimes a barbarism. Thus râjasic is used for râjasa.

To further aid the careful student, original terms are sometimes added in foot-notes, where they seem to clarify the meaning. The epithets applied to Shrî Krishna and Arjuna—the variety of which is so characteristic of Sanskrit conversation—are for the most part left untranslated, as being musical they thus add to the literary charm, whereas the genius of English is so different from that of Sanskrit, that the many-footed epithets become sometimes almost grotesque in translation. Names derived from that of an ancestor, as Pârtha, meaning the son of Prithâ, Kaunteya, meaning the son of Kuntî, are used in one form or the other, according to the rhythm of the sentence.

One other trifling matter, which is yet not trifling if it aids the student; when Âtmâ means the One Self, the SELF of all, it is printed in small capitals; where it means the lower, the personal self, it is printed in ordinary type; this is done because there is sometimes a play on the word, and it is difficult for an untrained reader to follow the meaning without some such assistance.

My wish, in adding this translation to those already before the public, was to preserve the spirit of the original, especially in its deeply devotional tone, while at the same time giving an accurate translation, reflecting the strength and the terseness of the Sanskrit. In order that mistakes, due to my imperfect knowledge, might be corrected, all of this translation has passed through the hands of one or other of the following gentlemen—friends of mine at Benares—to whom I here tender my grateful acknowledgments: Bâbus Pramada Das Mittra, Ganganath Jha, Kali Charan Mittra, and Upendranath Basu. A few of the notes are also due to them.

ANNIE BESANT.

THE BHAGAVAD GÎTÂ.

THE LORD'S SONG.

FIRST DISCOURSE.

AUM!

Dhritarâshtra said:

On the holy plain, on Kurukshetra, gathered together, eager for battle, what did they do, O Sanjaya, my people and the Pândavas? (1)

Sanjaya said:

Having seen arrayed the army of the Pândavas, the Râjâ Duryodhana approached his teacher,[1] and spake these words: (2)

[1] Drona, the son of Bharadvâja.

"Behold this mighty host of the sons of Pându, O teacher, arrayed by the son of Drupada, thy wise disciple. (3)

Heroes are these, mighty bowmen, to Bhîma and Arjuna equal in battle; Yuyudhâna, Virâta, and Drupada of the great car:[1] (4)

Drishtaketu, Chekitêna and the Râjâ of Kâshî, the valiant; Purujit and Khuntibhoja, and Shaivya, bulls[2] among men; (5)

Yudhâmanyu the strong, and Uttomauja the brave; Saubhadra and the Draupadeyas,[3] all of great cars. (6)

Know all those who are the chief of ours, O best of the twice-born, the leaders of my army; these I name to thee for thy information: (7)

[1] Leader of ten thousand bowmen.

[2] The bull, as the emblem of manly strength and vigour, is often used an epithet of honour.

[3] The son of Subhadrâ, Krishna's sister, and Arjuna, and the sons of Drupadi by the five sons of Pându.

Thou, Lord, and Bhîshma, and Karna ıd Kripa, conquering in battle; Ashtthâmâ, Vikarna, and Saumadatti[1] also; (8)

And many others, heroes, ready for my sake to give up their lives, trained in divers weapons and missiles and all well-skilled in war. (9)

Yet insufficient seems this army of ours, though commanded by Bhîshma, while sufficient seems that army of theirs, commanded even by Bhîma;[2] (10)

Therefore in the rank and file let all, standing firmly in their respective divisions, support Bhîshma, even all ye Generals." (11)

To enhearten him, the ancient of the

[1] The son of Somadatti.

[2] The commentators differ in their interpretation of this verse; Anandagiri takes it to mean just the reverse of Shridhata Svâmi, and connects "Aparyâptam" with the army of the Pândavas.

Kurus, the grandsire,[1] the glorious, blew his conch, sounding on high a lion's roar. (12)

Then conches and kettledrums, tabors and trumpets and cowhorns, suddenly blared forth, and the sound was an uproar. (13)

Then stationed in their great war-chariot, yoked to white horses, Mâdhava[2] and the son of Pându[3] blew their divine conches, (14)

Pânchajanya by Hrishîkesha, and Devadatta by Dhananjaya.[4] Vrikodara,[5] the terrible in action, blew his mighty conch, Paundra; (15)

[1] Bhishma.

[2] Shrî Krishna.

[3] Arjuna.

[4] Pânchajanya, Shrî Krishna's conch, was made from the bones of the giant Panchajana, slain by him; the title Hrishîkesha is "Lord of the senses." Dhananjaya, the "conqueror of wealth," is a title often given to Arjuna, whose conch is the "God-given."

[5] Bhîma; the meaning of the name of his conch is doubtful.

The Râjâ, the son of Kuntî, Yudhishthira, [blew] Anantavïjaya; Nakula and Sahadeva, Sughosha and Manipushpaka.[1] (16)

And Kâshya,[2] chief of bowmen, and Shikandin of the great car, Drishtadyumna and Virâta and Sâtyaki, the unconquered, (17)

Drupada and the Draupadeyas, O Lord of earth, and Saubhadra, the great-armed, on all sides their several conches blew. (18)

That tumult pierced the hearts of the sons of Dhritarâshtra, for truly the uproar re-echoed from earth and sky. (19)

Then beholding the sons of Dhritarâshtra standing arrayed, and the flight of missiles about to begin, he whose crest is an ape, the son of Pându, took up his bow, (20)

[1] The conches of the remaining three brothers were named respectively, "endless victory," "honey-tone" and "jewel-blossom."

[2] The king of Kâshi, the modern Benares.

And spake this word to Hrishîkesha, O Lord of earth.

(Arjuna said:)

"In the midst, between the two armies, my chariot stay, O Achyuta,[1] (21)

While I behold these standing, longing for battle, with whom I must strive in this tremendous war, (22)

And gaze on those here gathered together, ready to fight, desirous of pleasing the evil-minded son of Dhritarâshtra." (23)

Sanjaya said:

Thus addressed by Gudâkesha,[2] Hrishîkesha, O Bhârata! stayed that best of chariots in the midst, between the two armies, (24)

Over against Bhîshma, Drona and all the rulers of the world, and said: "O

[1] The changeless, the immovable.

[2] The lord of sleep, Arjuna.

Pârtha, behold these Kurus gathered together." (25)

Then saw Pârtha standing there uncles and grandfathers, teachers, mother's brothers, cousins, (their) sons and grandsons, comrades, (26)

Fathers-in-law and benefactors also in both armies; seeing all these kinsmen, thus standing arrayed, Kaunteya,[1] (27)

Deeply moved to pity, this uttered in sadness:

Arjuna said:

Seeing these my kinsmen arrayed, O Krishna, eager to fight, (28)

My limbs fail and my mouth is parched, my body quivers and my hair stands on end, (29)

Gândîva slips from my hand, and my skin burns all over, I am not able to stand, and my mind seems whirling, (30)

[1] The son of Kuntî, Arjuna.

And I see adverse omens, O Keshava.[1] Nor do I foresee any advantage from slaying kinsmen in battle. (31)

For I desire not victory, O Krishna, nor kingdom, nor pleasures; what is kingdom to us, O Govinda, what enjoyment, or even life? (32)

Those for whose sake we desire kingdom, enjoyments and pleasures, they stand here in battle, abandoning life and riches— (33)

Teachers, fathers, sons, as well as grandfathers, mother's brothers, fathers-in-law, grandsons, brothers-in-law, and other relatives. (34)

These I do not wish to kill, though [myself] slain, O Madhusûdana,[2] even for the sake of the kingship of the three worlds; how then for earth! (35)

Slaying these sons of Dhritarâshtra,

[1] An epithet, said by some to refer to hair—hairy.

[2] The slayer of Madhu, a demon.

what pleasure may be ours, O Janârdana?[1] killing these felons sin will but take hold of us. (36)

Therefore we should not kill the sons of Dhritarâshtra, our relatives; for how, killing our kinsmen, may we be happy, O Mâdhava? (37)

Although these, with intelligence overpowered by greed, see no guilt in the destruction of a family, no crime in hostility to friends, (38)

Why should we not learn to turn away from such a sin, O Janârdana, seeing the evils in the destruction of a family? (39)

In the destruction of a family the immemorial family dharmas[2] perish; in the perishing of dharma, lawlessness overcomes the whole family; (40)

[1] "Destroyer of the people." Shri Krishna as the conquering warrior against all forms of evil.

[2] Dharma is a wide word, primarily meaning the essential nature of a thing; hence, the laws of its being, its duty: and it includes religious rites, appropriate to those laws.

Owing to predominance of lawlessness, O Krishna, the women of the family become corrupt; women corrupted, O Vârshneya,[1] there ariseth caste-confusion; (41)

This confusion draggeth to hell the family-slaughterers, and the family, for their ancestors fall, deprived of rice-balls and libations. (42)

By these caste-confusing misdeeds of the family-slaughterers, the eternal caste Dharma and family Dharma are abolished. (43)

Of the men whose family Dharma is extinguished, O Janârdana, the abode is everlastingly in hell. Thus have we heard. (44)

Alas! in committing a great sin are we engaged, we who are endeavouring to kill our kindred from greed of the pleasures of kingship. (45)

If the sons of Dhritarâshtra, weapon-

[1] Belonging to the family of Vrishni.

in-hand, should slay me, unresisting, unarmed, in the battle, that would for me be the better. (46)

Sanjaya said:

Having thus spoken on the battle-[field], Arjuna sank down on the seat of the chariot, casting away his bow and arrow, his mind overborne by grief. (47)

Thus in the glorious Upanishad of the BHAGAVAD GÎTÂ, the science of Brahman, the scripture of Yoga, the dialogue between Shrî-Krishna and Arjuna, the first discourse, entitled:

THE DESPONDENCY OF ARJUNA.

SECOND DISCOURSE.

Sanjaya said:

To him thus with pity overcome, with smarting brimming eyes, despondent, Madhusûdana spake these words (1)

The Blessed Lord said:

Whence hath this dejection befallen thee in this perilous strait, ignoble,[1] Svarga-closing,[2] infamous, O Arjuna? (2)

Yield not to impotence, O Pârtha! it doth not befit thee. Shake off this paltry faint-heartedness! Stand up, Parantapa![3] (3)

[1] Literally, un-âryan.

[2] Literally, non-svargan; cowardice in the Kshattriya closed on him the door of Svarga, heaven.

[3] Conqueror of foes.

Arjuna said:

How, Madhusûdana, shall I attack with arrows in battle Bhîshma and Drona, worthy of reverence, O slayer of foes! (4)

Better to eat in this world even the beggars' crust than to slay these Gurus, high-minded. Slaying these Gurus, well-wishers,[1] I should taste of blood besprinkled feasts. (5)

Nor know I which for us would be the better, that we conquer them or they conquer us—these, whom having slain we should not care to live, even these arrayed against us, the sons of Dhritarâshtra. (6)

My heart is weighed down with the vice of faintness; my mind is confused as to Dharma.[2] I ask thee which may

[1] More often translated, "greedy of wealth," but the word is used elsewhere for well-wisher, and the term is more in accordance with the tone of Arjuna's remarks.

[2] Dharma is the *inner* nature of a thing, that

be the better—that tell me decisively. I am thy disciple, suppliant to thee; teach me. (7)

For I see not that it would drive away this anguish that withers up my senses, if I should attain monarchy on earth without a foe, or even the sovereignty of the Gods. (8)

Sanjaya said:

Gudâkesha, conqueror of his foes, having thus addressed Hrishîkesha, and said to Govinda, "I will not fight!" became silent. (6)

Then Hrishîkesha, tenderly smiling, O Bhârata, in the midst of the two armies, to him, despondent, spake these words: (10)

The Blessed Lord said:

Thou grievest for those that should

which makes it to be what it is externally. It is often translated law, duty, religion, but the essential idea is that of an inner life or law, the other meaning being subsidiary.

not be grieved for, yet speakest words of wisdom.[1] The wise grieve neither for the living nor for the dead. (11)

Nor at any time verily was I not, nor thou, nor these princes of men, nor verily shall we ever cease to be, hereafter. (12)

As the dweller in the body findeth in the body childhood, youth and old age, so passeth he on to another body; the steadfast one grieveth not thereat, (13)

The contacts of the senses, O son of Kuntî, giving cold and heat, pleasure and pain, they come and go, impermanent; endure them bravely, O Bhârata. (14)

The man whom these torment not, O chief of men, balanced in pain and pleasure, steadfast, he is fitted for immortality. (15)

The unreal hath no being; the real

[1] Words that sound wise but miss the deeper sense of wisdom.

never ceaseth to be; the truth about both hath been perceived by the seers of the Essence of things.[1] (16)

Know THAT to be indestructible by whom all this is pervaded. Nor can any work the destruction of that imperishable One. (17)

These bodies of the embodied One, who is eternal, indestructible, and boundless, are known as finite. Therefore fight, O Bhârata. (18)

He who regardeth this as a slayer, and he who thinketh he is slain, both of them are ignorant. He slayeth not, nor is he slain. (19)

He is not born, nor doth he die: nor having been, ceaseth he any more to be; unborn, perpetual, eternal and ancient, he is not slain when the body is slaughtered. (20)

Who knoweth him indestructible, perpetual, unborn, undiminishing, how

[1] Tattva. [2] The dweller in the body.

can that man slay, O Pârtha, or cause to be slain? (21)

As a man, casting off worn-out garments, taketh new ones, so the dweller in the body, casting off worn-out bodies, entereth into others that are new. (22)

Weapons cleave him not, nor fire burneth him, nor waters wet him, nor wind drieth him away. (23)

Uncleavable he, incombustible he, and indeed neither to be wetted nor dried away; perpetual, all-pervasive, stable, immovable, ancient, (24)

Unmanifest, unthinkable, immutable, he is called; therefore knowing him as such, thou shouldst not grieve. (25)

Or if thou thinkest of him as constantly being born and constantly dying, even then, O mighty-armed, thou shouldst not grieve. (26)

For certain is death for the born, and

certain birth for the dead; therefore over the inevitable thou shouldst not grieve. (27)

Beings are unmanifest in their origin, manifest in their midmost state, O Bhârata, unmanifest likewise are they in dissolution. What room then for lamentation? (28)

As marvellous one regardeth him; as marvellous another speaketh thereof; as marvellous another heareth thereof; yet having heard, none indeed understandeth. (29)

This dweller in the body of everyone is ever invulnerable, O Bhârata; therefore thou shouldst not grieve for any creature. (30)

Further, looking to thine own Dharma, thou shouldst not tremble; for there is nothing more welcome to a Kshattriya than righteous war. (31)

Happy the Kshattriyas, O Pârtha, who obtain such a fight, spontaneously offered as an open door to Svarga. (32)

But if thou wilt not carry on this righteous warfare, then, casting away thine own Dharma and thine honour, thou wilt incur sin. (33)

Men will recount thy perpetual dishonour, and, to one highly esteemed dishonour is worse than death. (34)

The great car-warriors[1] will think thou hast fled the battle from fear, and thou that wast highly thought of by them, wilt be lightly held. (35)

Many unseemly words will be spoken by thine enemies, slandering thy strength; what more painful than that; (36)

Slain, thou wilt obtain Svarga; victorious, thou wilt enjoy the earth; therefore stand up, O son of Kuntî, resolute to fight. (37)

Taking as equal pleasure and pain

[1] The generals.

gain and loss, victory and defeat, gird thee for the battle; thus thou shalt not incur sin. (38)

This teaching set forth to thee is in accordance with the Sânkhya; hear it now according to Yoga, imbued with which teaching, O Pârtha, thou shalt cast away the bonds of action. (39)

In this there is no loss of effort, nor is there transgression. Even a little of this Dharma frees one from great fear. (40)

The determinate reason is but one in this mortal life, O joy of the Kurus; many-branched and endless are the thoughts of the irresolute. (41)

Flowery speech is uttered by the foolish, rejoicing in the letter of the Vedas, O Pârtha, saying: "There is naught but this." (42)

With Kâma for self,[1] with Svarga for

[1] Those whose very self is Kâma, *i.e.*, desire, and who therefore act with a view to win Svarga, and also rebirth to wealth and rank.

goal, they offer birth as the fruit of action, and prescribe many and various ceremonies for the attainment of pleasure and lordship. (43)

For them who cling to pleasure and lordship, whose minds are captivated by such (speech), is not designed this (determinate) reason, on contemplation[1] steadily bent. (44)

The Vedas deal with the three attributes;[2] be thou above these three attributes, O Arjuna; beyond the pairs of opposites, ever steadfast in Sattva, careless of possessions, full of the SELF. (45)

All the Vedas are as useful to an enlightened Brâhman, as is a tank in a place covered all over with water. (46)

Thy business is with the action only,

[1] Samâdhi.

[2] Gunas=attributes, or forms of energy. They are Sattva, purity, Rajas, activity or passion, Tama, inertness or darkness.

never with its fruits; so let not the fruit of action be thy motive, nor be thou to inaction attached. (47)

Perform action, O Dhananjaya, dwelling in union with the divine,[1] renouncing attachments, and balanced evenly in success and failure: equilibrium is called Yoga. (48)

Far lower than Buddhi-Yoga[2] is action, O Dhananjaya. Take thou refuge in Buddhi; pitiable are they who work for fruit. (49)

United to Buddhi, one abandoneth here both good and evil deeds, therefore cleave thou to Yoga; Yoga is skill in action. (50)

The sages, united to Buddhi, renounce the fruit which action yieldeth, and liberated from the bonds of birth, they go to the blissful seat. (51)

[1] Dwelling in Yoga.

[2] Union with Buddhi; the innermost sheath (or vehicle) of Atmâ.

When thy Buddhi shall pass beyond this tangle of delusion, then thou shalt rise to indifference as to what has been heard and shall be heard. (52)

When thy Buddhi, bewildered by the Shruti,[1] shall stand immovable, fixed in contemplation then shalt thou attain to Yoga.[2] (53)

Arjuna said:

What is the mark of him who is stable of mind, steadfast in contemplation, O Keshava? how doth the stable-minded talk, how doth he sit, how walk? (54)

The Blessed Lord said:

When a man abandoneth, O Pârtha! all the desires of the heart, and is satisfied in the SELF by the SELF, then is he called stable in mind. (55)

[1] Revealed Scriptures.

[2] To union with Atmâ, the SELF; Yoga, or union, means harmony with the divine will. The word translated contemplation is, as before, Samâdhi.

He whose Manas is free from anxiety amid pains, indifferent amid pleasures, loosed from passion, fear and anger, he is called a Muni [1] of stable mind. (56)

He who on every side is without attachments, whatever hap of fair and foul, who neither likes nor dislikes, of such a one the understanding is well-poised. (57)

When, again, as a tortoise draws in on all sides its limbs, he withdraws his senses from the objects of sense, then is his understanding well-poised. (58)

The objects of sense, but not the taste (for them),[2] turn away from an abstemious dweller in the body; and even taste turneth away from him after the Supreme is seen. (59)

O son of Kuntî, the excited senses of

[1] A saint: in its original meaning one who observed the vow of silence.

[2] The objects turn away when rejected, but still desire for them remains; even desire is lost when the Supreme is seen.

(even) a wise man, though careful, impetuously carry away his Manas. (60)

Having restrained them all, he should sit harmonized, devoted wholly to me; for whose senses are mastered, of him the understanding is well-poised. (61)

Man, musing on the objects of sense, conceiveth an attachment to these; from attachment ariseth desire; from desire anger[1] cometh forth; (62)

From anger proceedeth delusion; from delusion confused memory; from confused memory the destruction of Buddhi;[2] from destruction of Buddhi, he perishes. (63)

But the disciplined self, moving among sense-objects with senses free from attraction and repulsion, mastered by the SELF, goeth to Peace. (64)

In that Peace the extinction of all pains ariseth for him, for of him whose

[1] Krodha.

[2] Discrimination.

heart is peaceful the Buddhi soon attaineth equilibrium. (65)

There is no Buddhi for the non-harmonized, nor for the non-harmonized is there concentration;[1] for him without concentration there is no peace, and for the unpeaceful how can there be happiness? (66)

Such of the roving senses as the Manas yieldeth to, that hurries away the understanding, just as the gale (hurries away) ships upon the waters. (67)

Therefore, O mighty-armed, whose senses are all completely restrained from the objects of sense, of him the understanding is well-poised. (68)

That which is the night of all beings, for the disciplined man is the time of waking; when other beings are waking, then is night for the Muni who seeth.[2] (69)

[1] Bhâvanâ.

[2] The sage is awake to things over which the

He attaineth Peace, into whom all desires flow as rivers flow into the ocean, which is filled with water but remaineth unmoved—not he who desireth desire. (70)

Whoso forsaketh all desires and goeth onwards free from yearnings, selfless and without egoism—he goeth to Peace. (71)

This is the Brahman state, O son of Prithâ. Having attained thereto none is bewildered. Who even at the death-hour is established therein, he goeth to the Nirvâna of Brahman. (72)

Thus in the glorious Upanishads of the BHAGAVAD GÎTÂ, the science of Brahman, the scripture of Yoga, the dialogue between Shrî Krishna and Arjuna, the second discourse, entitled:

YOGA BY THE SANKHYA.

ordinary man sleeps, and *vice versâ* the eyes of the sage are open to truths shut out from the common vision, while that which is real for the masses is illusion for the sage.

THIRD DISCOURSE.

Arjuna said:

If it be thought by thee that knowledge is superior to action, O Janârdana, why dost thou, O Keshava! enjoin on me this terrible action? (1)

With these perplexing words thou only confusest my understanding;[1] therefore tell me with certainty the one (way) by which I may reach bliss? (2)

The Blessed Lord said:

In this world there is a twofold path, as I before said, O sinless one, that of Yoga by knowledge—of the Sânkhyas, and that of Yoga by action—of the Yogîs. (3)

[1] Buddhi.

Man winneth not freedom from action by abstaining from activity, nor by mere renunciation (of activity) doth he rise to perfection. (4)

Nor can anyone, even for an instant, remain actionless; for helplessly is everyone driven to action by the energies[1] born of nature.[2] (5)

Who sitteth, controlling the organs of action, but dwelling in his mind on the objects of the senses, that bewildered man is called a hypocrite. (6)

But who, controlling the senses by Manas, O Arjuna, with the organs of action without attachment, performeth Yoga by action,[3] he is worthy. (7)

Perform thou right action, for action is superior to inaction, and, inactive,

[1] Guna.

[2] Prakriti.

[3] Karma-Yoga is the consecration of physical energy on the Divine Altar; *i.e.*, the using of one's organs of action simply in service, in obedience to Law and Duty.

even the maintenance of thy body would not be possible. (8)

The world is bound by action, unless performed for the sake of sacrifice; with such object, free from attachment, O son of Kuntî, perform thou action. (9)

Having in ancient times emanated mankind together with sacrifice, the Lord of emanation[1] said: "By this shall ye propagate; be this to you the Kâmadhuk;[2] (10)

"With this nourish ye the Gods, and may the Gods nourish you; thus nourishing one another, ye shall reap the supremest good. (11)

"For, nourished by sacrifice, the Gods shall bestow on you the enjoyments you desire." A thief verily is

[1] Prajâpati.

[2] The cow of Indra, from which each could milk what he wished for, hence the giver of desired objects.

he who enjoyeth what is given by Them without returning the gift. (12)

The righteous, who eat the remains of the sacrifice, are freed from all sins; but the impious, who dress food for their own sakes, they verily eat sin. (13)

From food creatures become; from rain is the production of food; rain proceedeth from sacrifice; sacrifice ariseth out of action; (14)

Know thou from Brahma[1] action groweth, and Brahma from the imperishable cometh. Therefore Brahman, the all-permeating, is ever present in sacrifice. (15)

He who on earth doth not follow the wheel thus revvoling, sinful of life and rejoicing in the senses, he, O son of Prithâ, liveth in vain. (16)

But the man verily who rejoiceth in

[1] An Indian of much knowledge translates Brahma here as "the Vedas."

the SELF, with the SELF is satisfied, and is content in the SELF, for him there is nothing to do; (17)

For him there is no interest in things done in this world, nor any in things not done, nor doth any object of his depend on any being. (18)

Therefore, without attachment, constantly perform action which is duty, for, performing action without attachment, man verily reacheth the Supreme. (19)

Janaka and others indeed attained to perfection by action; then having an eye to the protection of the masses also, thou shouldst perform action. (20)

Whatsoever a great man doeth, that other men also do; the standard he setteth up, by that the people go. (21)

There is nothing in the three worlds, O Pârtha, that should be done by Me, nor anything unattained that might be attained; yet I mingle in action. (22)

For if I mingled not ever in action, unwearied, men all around would follow My path, O son of Prithâ. (23)

These worlds would fall into ruin, if I did not perform action; I should be the author of confusion of castes, and should destroy these creatures. (24)

As the ignorant act from attachment to action, O Bhârata, so should the wise act without attachment, desiring the maintenance of mankind. (25)

Let no wise man unsettle the mind of ignorant people attached to action; but acting in harmony (with Me) let him render all action attractive. (26)

All actions are wrought by the energies of nature only. The self, deluded by egoism,[1] thinketh: "I am the doer." (27)

But he, O mighty-armed, who knoweth the essence of the divisions of the energies and functions, holding that

[1] Ahankâra, the separate "I am."

"the energies move amid the energies"[1] is not bound. (28)

Those deluded by the energies of nature are attached to the functions of the energies. The man of perfect knowledge should not unsettle the foolish whose knowledge is imperfect. (29)

Surrendering all actions to Me, with thy thoughts (resting) on the supreme SELF, from hope and egoism freed, and of mental fever cured, engage in battle. (30)

Who abide ever in this teaching of Mine, full of faith and free from cavilling, they too are released from actions. (31)

Who carp at My teaching and act not thereon, senseless, deluded in all knowledge, know thou them to be given over to destruction. (32)

[1] The energies as sense-organs move amid the energies as sense-objects. A suggested reading is "The functions dwell in the propensities."

Even the man of knowledge acteth according to his own nature; beings follow nature; what shall restraint avail? (33)

Affection and aversion for the objects of sense abide in the senses; let none come under the dominion of these two; they are his adversaries. (34)

Better one's own Dharma, though destitute of merit than the Dharma of another, well-discharged. Better death in the discharge of one's own Dharma; the Dharma of another is full of danger. (35)

Arjuna said:

But dragged on by what does a man commit sin, reluctantly indeed, O Vârshneya, as it were by force constrained? (36)

The Blessed Lord said:

It is desire, it is wrath, begotten by the Rajas-energy; all-consuming, all-polluting, know thou this as our foe here on earth. (37)

4

As a flame is enveloped by smoke, as a mirror by dust, as an embryo is wrapped by the womb, so This[1] is enveloped by it. (38)

Enveloped is wisdom by this constant enemy of the wise in the form of desire, which is insatiable as a flame. (39)

The senses, Manas and Buddhi are said to be its seat; by these enveloping wisdom, it bewilders the dweller in the body. (40)

Therefore, O best of the Bhâratas, mastering first the senses, do thou slay this thing of sin, destructive of wisdom and knowledge! (41)

It is said that the senses are great; greater than the senses is Manas; greater than Manas is Buddhi; but what is greater than Buddhi, is He.[2] (42)

[1] The universe: "This" as opposed to "THAT," the Eternal. Some say "This" stands for "knowledge."

[2] The Supreme.

Thus understanding Him as greater than Buddhi, restraining the self by the SELF, slay thou, O mighty-armed, the enemy in the form of desire, difficult to overcome. (43)

Thus in the glorious Upanishads of the BHAGAVAD GÎTÂ, the science of Brahman, the scripture of Yoga, the dialogue between Shrî Krishna and Arjuna, the third discourse, entitled:

THE YOGA OF ACTION.

FOURTH DISCOURSE.

The Blessed Lord said:

This imperishable Yoga I declared to Vivasvat; Vivasvat taught it to Manu; Manu to Ikshvâku told it! (1)

This, handed on down the line, the King-Sages knew. This Yoga by great efflux of time decayed in the world, O Parantapa. (2)

This same ancient Yoga hath been to-day declared to thee by Me, for thou art My devotee and My friend; it is the Supreme Secret. (3)

Arjuna said:

Later was thy birth, earlier the birth of Vivasvat; how then am I to understand that Thou declarest it in the beginning? (4)

The Blessed Lord said:

Many births have been left behind by Me and by thee, O Arjuna. I know them all, but thou knowest not thine, Parantapa. (5)

Though unborn, the imperishable SELF, and also the Lord of all beings, brooding over nature, which is Mine own, yet I am born through My own Mâyâ.[1] (6)

Whenever there is decay of Dharma, O Bhârata, and there is exaltation of Adharma,[2] then I Myself come forth; (7)

For the protection of the good, for the destruction of evil-doers, for the sake of firmly establishing Dharma, I am born from age to age. (8)

[1] The power of thought that produces form, which is transient and therefore unreal compared with the eternal Reality; hence Mâyâ comes to be taken as the power of producing illusion.

[2] The opposite of dharma, all that is disorderly against the nature of things.

He who thus knoweth My divine birth and action, in its essence, having abandoned the body, cometh not to birth again, but cometh unto Me, O Arjuna. (9)

Freed from passion, fear and anger, thinking on Me, taking refuge in Me, purified in the fire of wisdom,[1] many have entered into My being. (10)

However men approach Me, even so do I accept them, for the path men take from every side is Mine, O Pârtha. (11)

They who long after success in action sacrifice on earth to the Gods; for in brief space verily, in this world of men, success is born of action. (12)

The four castes were emanated by Me, by the different distribution of energies and actions; know Me to be the author of them, though the actionless and inexhaustible. (13)

[1] Tapas, from Tap, blazing like fire.

Nor do actions affect Me, nor is the fruit of action desired by Me. He who thus knoweth Me is not bound by actions. (14)

Having thus known, our forefathers, ever seeking liberation, performed action; therefore do thou also perform action, as did our forefathers in the olden time. (15)

"What is action, what inaction?" Even the wise are herein perplexed. Therefore I will declare to thee the action by knowing which thou shalt be loosed from evil. (16)

It is needful to discriminate action, to discriminate unlawful action, and to discriminate inaction; mysterious is the path of action. (17)

He who seeth inaction in action, and action in inaction, he is wise among men, he is harmonious, even while performing all action. (18)

Whose works are all free from the

moulding of desire, whose actions are burned up by the fire of wisdom, him the wise have called a Sage. (19)

Having abandoned attachment to the fruit of action, always content, nowhere seeking refuge, he is not doing anything, although doing actions. (20)

Hoping for naught, his mind and self controlled, having abandoned all greed, performing action by the body alone, he doth not commit sin. (21)

Content with whatsoever he obtaineth without effort, free from the pairs of opposites, without envy, balanced in success and failure, though acting he is not bound; (22)

Of one with attachment dead, harmonious, with his thoughts established in wisdom, working for sacrifice (only), all action melts away. (23)

Brahman the oblation, Brahman the clarified butter, are offered to Brahman the fire, by Brahman; unto Brahman verily shall he go who in his action meditateth wholly upon Brahman. (24)

Some Yogîs offer up sacrifice to the Gods;[1] others sacrifice only by pouring sacrifice into the fire of Brahman; (25)

Some pour as sacrifice hearing and the other senses into the fires of restraint; some pour sound and the other objects of sense into the fires of the senses as sacrifice; (26)

Others again into the wisdom-kindled fire of union (attained) by self-control, pour as sacrifice all the functions of the senses and the functions of life; (27)

Yet others the sacrifice of wealth, the sacrifice of austerity, the sacrifice of Yoga, the sacrifice of silent reading and wisdom, men concentrated and of effectual vows; (28)

Yet others pour as sacrifice the outgoing breath in the incoming, and the incoming in the outgoing, restraining

[1] Literally, divine sacrifice.

the flow of the outgoing and incoming breaths, solely absorbed in Prânâyâma;[1] (29)

Others, regular in food, pour as sacrifice their life breaths in life breaths. All these are knowers of sacrifice, and by sacrifice have destroyed their sins. (30)

The eaters of the amrita[2] remains of sacrifices go to the eternal Brahman. This world is not for the non-sacrificer, much less the other, O best of the Kurus. (31)

Many and various sacrifices are thus spread out before Brahman.[3] Know thou that all these are born of action, and thus knowing thou shalt be free. (32)

[1] Restraint of breath, a technical name for this practice.

[2] Amrita is the elixir of immortality, and the amrita-remains, therefore, are foods that give immortality.

[3] "In the Vedas" is another interpretation.

Better than the sacrifice of any objects is the sacrifice of wisdom, O Parantapa. All actions in their entirety, O Pârtha, culminate in wisdom. (33)

Learn thou this by discipleship,[1] by investigation, and by service. The wise, the seers of the Essence of things, will instruct thee in wisdom, (34)

And having known this, thou shalt not again fall into this confusion, O Pândàva; for by this thou wilt see all beings without exception in the SELF and thus in Me. (35)

Even if thou art the most sinful of all sinners, yet shalt thou cross over all sin by the raft of wisdom. (36)

As the burning fire reduces fuel to ashes, O Arjuna, so doth the fire of wisdom reduce all actions to ashes. (37)

Verily there is nothing so pure in

[1] Literally, falling at the feet, *i.e.*, the feet of the teacher.

this world as wisdom; he that is perfected in Yoga finds it in the SELF in due season. (38)

The man who is full of faith[1] obtaineth wisdom, and he also who hath mastery over his senses, and having obtained wisdom he goeth swiftly to the Supreme Peace. (39)

But the ignorant, faithless, doubting self goeth to destruction; nor this world nor that beyond nor happiness is there for the doubting self. (40)

He who hath renounced actions by Yoga, who hath cloven asunder doubt by wisdom, who is ruled by the SELF,[2] actions do not bind him, O Dhananjaya. (41)

Therefore, with the sword of the wisdom of the SELF cleaving asunder this ignorance-born doubt, dwelling in

[1] Who is intent upon faith.

[2] Madhusûdana explains *âtmavantam* as "always watchful."

thy heart, be established in Yoga. Stand up, O Bhârata! (42)

Thus in the glorious Upanishads of the BHAGAVAD GÎTÂ, the science of Brahman, the scripture of Yoga, the dialogue between Shrî Krishna and Arjuna, the fourth discourse, entitled:

THE YOGA OF WISDOM.

FIFTH DISCOURSE.

Arjuna said:

Renunciation of actions, thou praisest, O Krishna, and then also Yoga. Of the two which one is the better? Tell me that conclusively. (1)

The Blessed Lord said:

Renunciation and Yoga by action both lead to the highest bliss; of the two, Yoga by action is verily better than renunciation of action. (2)

He should be known as a perpetual Sannyâsî,[1] who neither hateth nor desireth; free from the pairs of opposites, O mighty-armed, he is easily set free from bondage. (3)

[1] An ascetic who renounces all.

Children, not Sages, speak of the Sânkhya and Yoga as different; he who is duly established in one obtaineth the fruits of both. (4)

That place which is gained by the Sânkhyas is reached by the Yogîs also. He seeth, who seeth that the Sânkhya and the Yoga are one. (5)

But without Yoga, O mighty-armed, renunciation is hard to attain to; the Yoga-harmonised Muni swiftly goeth to Brahman. (6)

He who is harmonised by Yoga, the self purified, SELF-ruled, the senses subdued, whose SELF is the SELF of all beings, although acting he is not affected. (7)

"I do not anything," should think the harmonised one, who knoweth the essence of things; seeing, hearing, touching, smelling, eating, moving, sleeping, breathing, (8)

Speaking, giving, grasping, opening

and closing the eyes, he holdeth: "The senses move among the objects of sense." (9)

He who acteth, placing all actions in Brahman, abandoning attachment, is unaffected by sin as a lotus leaf by the waters. (10)

Yogîs, having abandoned attachment, perform action only by the body, by Manas, by Buddhi, and even by the senses, for the purification of the self. (11)

The harmonised man, having abandoned the fruit of action, attaineth to everlasting Peace; the non-harmonised, impelled by desire, attached to fruit, are bound. (12)

Mentally renouncing all actions, the sovereign dweller in the body resteth serenely in the nine-gated city,[1] neither acting nor causing to act. (13)

The Lord of the world produceth not

[1] The body, often called the city of Brahman.

the idea of agency, nor actions, nor the union together of action and its fruit; nature, however, energiseth. (14)

The Lord accepteth neither the evil nor yet the well-doing of any. Wisdom is enveloped by unwisdom; therewith mortals are deluded. (15)

Verily, in whom unwisdom is destroyed by the wisdom of the SELF, in them wisdom, shining as the sun, reveals the Supreme. (16)

Thinking on THAT, merged in THAT, established in THAT, solely devoted to THAT, they go whence there is no return, their sins dispelled by wisdom. (17)

Sages look equally on a Brâhman adorned with learning and humility, a cow, an elephant, and even a dog, and a Svapâka.[1] (18)

Even here on earth everything is overcome by those whose Manas re-

[1] The lowest class of outcasts.

mains balanced; Brahman is incorruptible and balanced; therefore they are established in Brahman. (19)

With Buddhi firm, unperplexed, the Brahman-knower, established in Brahman, neither rejoiceth on obtaining what is pleasant, nor sorroweth on obtaining what is unpleasant. (20)

He whose self is unattached to external contacts and findeth joy in the SELF, having the self harmonised with Brahman by Yoga, enjoys happiness exempt from decay. (21)

The delights that are contact-born they are verily wombs of pain, for they have beginning and ending, O Kaunteya; not in them may rejoice the wise. (22)

He who is able to endure here on earth, ere he be liberated from the body, the propulsive force arising from desire and passion, he is harmonised, he is a happy man. (23)

He who is happy within, who rejoiceth within, who is illuminated within, that Yogî, becoming Brahman, goeth to the Brahma-Nirvâna. (24)

The Rishis, their sins destroyed, their duality removed, their selves controlled, intent upon the welfare of all beings, obtain the Brahma. (25)

Brahma-Nirvâna lies near to those who know themselves, who are disjoined from desire and passion, subdued in nature, of subdued thoughts. (26)

Having external contacts excluded, and with gaze fixed between the eyebrows; having made the outgoing and incoming breaths equal, moving within the nostrils, (27)

With senses, Manas and Buddhi ever controlled, solely pursuing liberation, the Muni, having for ever cast away desire, fear and passion, he verily is liberated. (28)

Having known Me, as the Lord of sacrifice and of austerity, the mighty Ruler of all the worlds, and the Lover of all beings, he goeth to Peace. (29)

Thus in the glorious Upanishads of the Bhagavad Gîtâ, the science of Brahman, in the scripture of Yoga, in the dialogue between Shrî Krishna and Ârjuna, the fifth discourse, entitled:

THE YOGA OF THE RENUNCIATION OF ACTION.

SIXTH DISCOURSE.

The Blessed Lord said:

He that performeth such action as is duty, independently of the fruit of action, he is a Sannyâsî, and he is a Yogî, not he that is without fire, and who doeth nothing.[1] (1)

That which is called renunciation know thou that as Yoga, O Pândava; nor doth any one become a Yogî with the formative will[2] unrenounced. (2)

For a Muni who is seeking Yoga, action is called the means; for the

[1] The Sannyâsi lights no sacrificial fire, and performs no sacrifices nor ceremonies; but merely to omit these, without true renunciation, is not to be a real Sannyâsi.

[2] The imaginative faculty, that makes plans for the future.

same Muni, when he is enthroned in Yoga, serenity is called the means. (3)

When a man feeleth no attachment either for the objects of sense or for actions, renouncing the formative will, then, he is said to be enthroned in Yoga. (4)

Let him raise the self by the SELF, and not let the self become depressed; for verily is the SELF the friend of the self, and also the SELF the self's enemy; (5)

The SELF is the friend of the self of him in whom the self by the SELF is vanquished; but to the unsubdued self,[1] the SELF verily becometh hostile as an enemy. (6)

The higher Self of him who is SELF-controlled and peaceful, is uniform in cold and heat, pleasure and pain, as well as in honour and dishonour. (7)

[1] Literally, the non-self.

The Yogî[1] who is satisfied with wisdom and knowledge unwavering, whose senses are subdued, to whom a lump of earth, a stone and gold are the same, is said to be harmonised. (8)

He is highly esteemed who regards impartially lovers, friends, and foes, strangers, neutrals, foreigners and relatives, also the righteous and unrighteous. (9)

Let the Yogî constantly engage himself in Yoga, remaining in a secret place by himself, with thought and self subdued, free from hope and greed. (10)

In a pure place, established on a fixed seat of his own, neither very much raised nor very low, made of a cloth, a black antelope skin and kusha grass, one over the other. (11)

There, having made Manas one-pointed, with thought and the functions

[1] The word Yogi is used for any one who is practising Yoga, as well as for the man who has attained union.

of the senses subdued, steady on his seat, he should practise Yoga for the purification of the self. (12)

Holding the body, head, and neck erect, immovably steady, looking fixedly at the point of the nose, with unwandering gaze, (13)

The self serene, fearless, firm in the vow of the Brahmachârî,[1] Manas controlled, thinking on Me, harmonised, let him sit aspiring after Me. (14)

The Yogî, ever united thus with the SELF, with Manas controlled, goeth to Peace, to the supreme Nirvâna that abideth in Me. (15)

Verily Yoga is not for him who eateth too much, nor who abstaineth to excess, nor who is too much addicted to sleep, nor even to wakefulness, O Arjuna. (16)

Yoga killeth out all pain for him who

[1] A Brahmachâri is a man who is keeping the vow of continence.

is regulated in eating and amusement, regulated in performing actions, regulated in sleeping and waking. (17)

When his subdued thought is fixed on the SELF, free from longing after all desirable things, then it is said, "he is harmonised." (18)

As a lamp sheltered from the wind flickereth not, to such is likened the Yogî of subdued thought, absorbed in the Yoga of the SELF. (19)

That in which the mind finds rest, quieted by the practice of Yoga, that in which he seeing the SELF by the SELF, in the SELF is satisfied; (20)

That in which he findeth the supreme delight which the Buddhi can grasp beyond the senses, wherein established, he moveth not from the Reality; (21)

Which, having obtained, he thinketh there is no greater gain beyond it; wherein established, he is not shaken even by heavy sorrow; (22)

That should be known by the name of Yoga, this disconnection from the union with pain. This Yoga must be clung to with a firm conviction and steady thoughts. (23)

Abandoning without reserve all desires born of the imagination, by Manas curbing in the aggregate of the senses on every side, (24)

Little by little let him gain tranquillity by means of Buddhi controlled by steadiness; having made Manas abide in the SELF, let him not think of anything. (25)

As often as the wavering and unsteady Manas goeth forth, so often reining it in, let him bring it under the control of the SELF. (26)

Supreme joy is for this Yogî whose Manas is peaceful, whose passion-nature is calmed, who is sinless and of the nature of Brahman. (27)

The Yogî who thus ever harmonising

the self with Brahman, hath put away sin, he easily enjoyeth the infinite bliss of contact with Brahman. (28)

The self, harmonised by Yoga, seeth the SELF abiding in all beings, all beings in the SELF; everywhere he seeth the same. (29)

He who seeth Me everywhere, and seeth everything in Me, of him will I never lose hold, and he shall never lose hold of Me. (30)

He who, established in unity, worshippeth Me, abiding in all beings, that Yogî liveth in Me, whatever his mode of living. (31)

He who, through the likeness of the SELF,[1] O Arjuna, seeth identity in everything, whether pleasant or painful, he is considered a perfect Yogî. (32)

Arjuna said:

This Yoga which Thou hast declared

[1] The same SELF shining in the heart of each.

to be by equanimity, O Madhusûdana, I see not a stable foundation for it, owing to restlessness; (33)

For Manas is verily restless, O Krishna; it is impetuous, strong and difficult to bend; I deem it as hard to curb as the wind. (34)

The Blessed Lord said:

Without doubt, O mighty-armed, Manas is hard to curb and restless; but it may be curbed by constant practice and by indifference. (35)

Yoga is hard to attain, methinks, by a self that is uncontrolled; but by the self-controlled it is attainable by properly directed energy. (36)

Arjuna said:

He who is unsubdued but who possesseth faith, with Manas wandering away from Yoga, failing to attain perfection in Yoga, what path doth he tread, O Krishna? (37)

Fallen from both, is he destroyed like a rent cloud, unsteadfast, O mighty-armed, deluded in the path of Brahman? (38)

Deign, O Krishna, to completely dispel this doubt of mine; for there is none to be found save thyself able to destroy this doubt. (39)

The Blessed Lord said:

O son of Prithâ, neither in this world nor in the life to come is there destruction for him; never doth any who worketh righteousness, O beloved, tread the path of woe. (40)

Having attained to the worlds of the pure-doing, and having dwelt there for eternal years, he who fell from Yoga is reborn in a pure and blessed house; (41)

Or he may even be born into a family of wise Yogîs; but such a birth as that is hard to obtain in this world. (42)

There he recovereth the characteristics belonging to his former body, and with these again laboureth for perfection, O joy of the Kurus! (43)

By that former practice he is irresistibly swept away. Only wishing to know Yoga, even the seeker after Yoga goeth beyond the Brâhmic word,[1] (44)

But the Yogî, labouring with assiduity, purified from sin, fully perfected through manifold births, he reacheth the supreme goal. (45)

The Yogî is greater than the ascetics; he is thought to be greater than even the wise; the Yogî is greater than the men of action; therefore become thou a Yogî, O Arjuna! (46)

And among all Yogîs, he who full of faith, with the inner SELF abiding in

[1] The Vedas.

Me, adoreth Me, he is considered by Me to be the most completely harmonised. (47)

Thus in the glorious Upanishads of the BHAGAVAD GÎTÂ, the science of Brahman, the scripture of Yoga, the dialogue between Shrî Krishna and Arjuna, the sixth discourse, entitled:

THE YOGA OF SELF-SUBDUAL.

SEVENTH DISCOURSE.

The Blessed Lord said:

With Manas clinging to Me, O Pârtha performing Yoga, refuged in Me, how thou shalt without doubt know Me to the uttermost, that hear thou. (1)

I will declare to thee this knowledge and wisdom in its completeness, which, having known, there is nothing more here remaineth to be known. (2)

Among thousands of men scarce one striveth for perfection; of the successful strivers scarce one knoweth Me in essence. (3)

Earth, water, fire, air, ether, Manas and Buddhi also and Ahankâra—these are the eightfold division of My Prakriti—[1] (4)

This the inferior. Know My other Prakriti, the higher, the life-element, O mighty-armed, by which the universe is upheld. (5)

Know this to be the womb of all beings. I am the going forth of the whole universe and likewise its dissolving. (6)

There is naught whatsoever higher than I, O Dhananjaya. All this is threaded on Me as jewels on a string. (7)

I the sapidity in waters, O Son of Kuntî, I the radiance in moon and sun; Pranava[2] in all the Vedas, sound in ether, and virility in men; (8)

The pure fragrance of earths and the brilliance in fire am I; the life in all

[1] Prakriti is matter in the widest sense of the term, including all that has extension.

[2] The sacred word Om.

beings, and I am the austerity in ascetics. (9)

Know Me, O Pârtha! as the eternal seed of all beings. I am the Buddhi of the Buddhi-endowed, the splendour of splendid things am I. (10)

And I the strength of the strong, devoid of desire and passion. In beings I am desire not contrary to Dharma, O Lord of the Bhâratas. (11)

The natures that are sâttvic, râjasic, tâmasic, these know as from Me; not I in them, but they in Me. (12)

All this world, deluded by these natures made by the three Gunas, knoweth not Me, above these, imperishable. (13)

This divine Mâyâ of Mine, Gunamade, is hard to pierce; they who come to Me, they cross over this Mâyâ. (14)

The evil-doing, the deluded, the vilest men, they come not to Me, they whose wisdom is destroyed by Mâyâ, who have embraced the nature of Asuras. (15)

Fourfold in division are the righteous ones who worship Me, O Arjuna: the suffering, the seeker for knowledge, the self-interested [and] the wise, O Lord of the Bhâratas. (16)

Of these, the wise, constantly harmonised, worshipping the One, is the best; I am supremely dear to the wise, and he is dear to Me. (17)

Noble are all these, but I hold the wise as verily Myself; he, SELF-united, is fixed on Me, the highest goal. (18)

At the close of many births the man full of wisdom cometh unto Me: "Vâsudeva[1] is all," saith he, the Mahâtmâ, very difficult to find. (19)

They whose wisdom hath been rent away by desires go forth to other Gods, resorting to various external

[1] A name for Krishna, as the son of Vasudeva.

observances, according to their own natures. (20)

Any devotee who seeketh to worship with faith any such aspect, I verily bestow the unswerving faith of that man. (21)

He, endowed with that faith, seeketh the worship of such a one, and from him he obtaineth his desires, I verily decreeing the benefits; (22)

Finite indeed the fruit; that belongeth to those who are of small intelligence. To the Gods go the worshippers of the Gods, but My devotees come unto Me. (23)

Those without Buddhi think of Me, the unmanifest, as having manifestation, knowing not My supreme nature, imperishable, most excellent. (24)

Nor am I of all discovered, enveloped in My Yoga-Mâyâ.[1] This deluded

[1] The creative power of Yoga, all things being the thought forms of the One.

world knoweth Me not, the unborn, the imperishable. (25)

I know the beings that are past, that are present, that are to come, O Arjuna, but no one knoweth Me. (26)

By the delusion of the pairs of opposites, sprung from attraction and repulsion, O Bhârata! all beings walk this universe wholly deluded, O Parantapa. (27)

But those men of pure deeds, in whom sin is come to an end, they freed from the delusive pairs of opposites, worship Me, steadfast in vows. (28)

They who refuged in Me strive for liberation from birth and death, they know Brahman, the whole Adhyâtma, and all Karma. (29)

They who know Me as Adhibhûta, as Adhidaiva and a Adhiyagnya[1] they,

[1] These five terms mean respectively the supreme SELF, Action, the supreme living being (in the sense of element, material for building a universe), the supreme God, the supreme

harmonized in mind, know Me verily even in the time of forthgoing.[1] (30)

Thus in the glorious Upanishads of the BHAGAVAD GÎTÂ, the science of Brahman, the scripture of Yoga, the dialogue between Shri Krishna and Arjuna, the seventh discourse, entitled:

THE YOGA OF DISCRIMINATIVE KNOWLEDGE.

sacrifice. The Sanskrit names are retained, lest the explanation given of them in the next discourse, by Shrî Krishna himself, should lose any of its force.

[1] Death—going forth from the body.

EIGHTH DISCOURSE.

Arjuna said:

What is that Brahman, what Adhyâtma, what Karma, O Purushottama? And what is declared Adhibhûta, what is called Adhidaiva? (1)

Who is Adhiyagnya in this body, and how, O Madhusûdana? And how at the time of forthgoing art thou known by the SELF-controlled? (2)

The Blessed Lord said:

The indestructible, the supreme, is Brahman; His essential nature is called Adhyâtmâ: the primal sacrifice that causes the birth of beings is named Karma; (3)

Adhibhûta is My perishable nature,

and Adhidaiva the life-giving energy;[1] Adhiyagnya am I, here in the body, O best of living beings. (4)

And he who, casting off the body, goeth forth thinking upon Me only at the time of the end, he entereth into My being: there is no doubt of that. (5)

Whosoever at the end abandoneth the body, thinking upon any being, to that only he goeth, O Kaunteya, ever to that conformed in nature. (6)

Therefore at all times think upon Me only, and fight. With Manas and Buddhi set on Me, without doubt thou shalt come to Me. (7)

With the mind not wandering after aught else, harmonised by continual practice, constantly meditating, O Pârtha, one goeth to the Purusha, supreme, divine. (8)

He who thinketh upon the Ancient,

[1] Purusha, the male creative energy.

the Omniscient, the All-Ruler, minuter than the atom, the supporter of all, of form unimaginable, refulgent as the sun beyond the darkness. (9)

In the time of forthgoing, with unshaken Manas, fixed in devotion, by the power of Yoga drawing together his life-breath in the centre of the two eyebrows, he goeth to this Purusha, supreme, divine. (10)

That which is declared indestructible by the Veda-knowers, that which the controlled and passion-free enter, that desiring which Brahmachârya[1] is performed, that path I will declare to thee with brevity. (11)

All the gates[2] closed, Manas confined in the heart, the life-breath fixed in his own head, firm in Yoga, (12)

"Om!" the one-syllabled Brahman,

[1] The vow of continence.

[2] The gates of the body, *i.e.*, the sense-organs.

reciting, thinking upon Me, he who goeth forth, abandoning the body, he goeth to the highest goal. (13)

He who constantly thinketh upon Me, not thinking ever of another, of him I am easily reached, O Pârtha, of this ever harmonised Yogî. (14)

Having come to Me, these Mahâtmâs come not again to birth, the place of pain, non-eternal; they have gone to the highest bliss. (15)

The worlds, beginning with the world of Brahmâ, they come and go, O Arjuna; but he who cometh unto Me, O Kaunteya, he knoweth birth no more. (16)

The people who know the day of Brahmâ, a thousand Yugas in duration, and the night, a thousand ages in ending, they know day and night. (17)

From the unmanifested all the manifested stream forth at the coming of day; at the coming of night they dissolve, even in That called the unmanifested. (18)

This multitude of beings, going forth repeatedly, is dissolved at the coming of night; by ordination, O Pârtha, it streams forth at the coming of day. (19)

Therefore verily there existeth, higher than that unmanifested, another unmanifested, eternal, which, in the destroying of all beings, is not destroyed. (20)

That unmanifested, "the Indestructible," It is called; It is named the highest goal. They who reach It return not. That is My supreme abode. (21)

He, the highest Purusha, O Pârtha, may be reached by unswerving devotion to Him alone, in whom all beings abide, by whom all This[1] is pervaded. (22)

That time wherein going forth, Yogîs

[1] This, the universe, in opposition to THAT, the source of all.

return not, and also that wherein going forth they return, that time shall I declare to thee, O prince of the Bhâratas. (23)

Fire, light, day-time, the bright fortnight, the six months of the northern path—then, going forth, the men who know Brahman go to Brahman. (24)

Smoke, night-time, the dark fortnight also, the six months of the southern path—then the Yogî, obtaining the moonlight,[1] returneth. (25)

Light and darkness, these are thought the world's eternal paths; by the one he goeth who returneth not, by the other he who returneth again. (26)

Knowing these paths, O Pârtha, the Yogî is nowise perplexed. Therefore in all times be firm in Yoga, O Arjuna. (27)

The fruit of meritorious deeds, at-

[1] The lunar, or astral, body. Until this is slain the soul returns to birth.

tached in the Vedas to sacrifices, to austerities, and also to almsgiving, the Yogî passeth all these by having known this, and goeth to the supreme and ancient Seat. (28)

Thus in the glorious Upanishads of the Bhagavad Gîtâ, the science of Brahman, the scripture of Yoga, the dialogue between Shri Krishna and Arjuna, the eighth discourse, entitled:

THE YOGA OF THE INDESTRUCTIBLE SUPREME BRAHMAN.

NINTH DISCOURSE.

The Blessed Lord said:

To thee, the uncarping, verily shall I declare this profoundest Secret, wisdom with knowledge combined, which, having known, thou shalt be freed from evil. (1)

Kingly Science, kingly Secret, supreme Purifier, this; experimental, according to Dharma, very easy to perform, imperishable. (2)

Men without faith in this Dharma, O Parantapa, not reaching Me, return to the paths of this mortal world. (3)

By Me all this world is pervaded, in My unmanifested aspect; all beings have root in Me, I am not rooted in them, (4)

Nor have beings root in Me; behold my sovereign Yoga! The support of beings yet not rooted in beings, My SELF their efficient cause. (5)

As the mighty air everywhere moving is rooted in the Âkâsha, so all beings rest rooted in me—thus know thou. (6)

All beings, O Kaunteya! go into my Prakriti at the end of a Kalpa;[1] at the beginning of a Kalpa I again send them out. (7)

Abiding Prakriti's Lord, I send forth again and again all this multitude of beings, helpless, by the force of Prakriti. (8)

Nor do these works bind me, O Dhananjaya, enthroned on high, unattached to these works. (9)

By My presiding, Prakriti sends forth the moving and unmoving; because of this, O Kaunteya, the universe revolves. (10)

[1] A period of activity, of manifestation.

The foolish disregard Me, when clad in human semblance, ignorant of My supreme nature, the great Lord of beings; (11)

Empty of hope, empty of deeds, empty of wisdom, senseless, partaking of the deceitful râkshasic and âsûric Prakriti.[1] (12)

Verily the Mahâtmâs, O Pârtha! partaking of My divine Prakriti, worship with Manas unwavering, having known Me, the imperishable source of beings. (13)

Always magnifying Me, strenuous, firm in vows, prostrating themselves before Me, they worship Me with devotion, ever harmonized. (14)

Others also sacrificing with the sacrifice of wisdom, worship Me as the One and the Manifold everywhere present. (15)

[1] The tâmasic Guna, or dark quality of Prakriti, characterises these demons.

I the oblation; I the sacrifice; I the ancestral offering; I the fire-giving herb; the mantram I; I also the butter; I the fire; the burnt-offering I; (16)

I the Father of this universe, the Mother, the Supporter, the Grandsire; the Holy One to be known, the Om-kâra, and also the Rig, Sâma, and Yajur. (17)

The Path, Husband, Lord, Witness, Abode, Shelter, Lover, Origin, Dissolution, Foundation, Treasure-house, Seed imperishable. (18)

I give heat; I hold back and send forth the rain; immortality and also death, Sat and Asat[1] am I, Arjuna. (19)

The knowers of the three,[2] the Soma-drinkers, the purified from sin, worshipping Me with sacrifice, pray of Me

[1] Existence and non-existence, the final pair of opposites, beyond which is only the One.

[2] Vedas.

the way to Svarga; they, ascending to the holy world of the God Indra, eat in heaven the divine feasts of the Gods. (20)

They, having enjoyed the spacious Svarga-world, their holiness withered,[1] come back to this mortal world. Following the virtues enjoined by the three,[2] desiring desires, they obtain the transitory. (21)

To those men who worship Me alone, thinking of no other, to those ever harmonious, I bring full security of Yoga. (22)

Even the devotees of other Gods, who worship full of faith, they also worship Me, O son of Kuntî, though contrary to the ancient rule. (23)

I am indeed the enjoyer of all sacrifices, and also the Lord, but they know

[1] The fruit of their good deeds finished, their reward exhausted.

[2] Vedas.

Me not in essence, and hence they fall. (24)

They who worship the Gods go to the Gods; to the Pitris go the Pitri-worshippers; to the Bhûtas go those who sacrifice to Bhûtas;[1] but My worshippers come unto Me. (25)

He who offereth to Me with devotion a leaf, a flower, a fruit, water, that I accept from the purified self, offered as it is with devotion. (26)

Whatsoever thou doest, whatsoever thou eatest, whatsoever thou offerest, whatsoever thou givest. whatsoever thou doest of austerity, O Kaunteya! do thou that as an offering unto Me. (27)

Thus shalt thou be liberated from the bonds of action (yielding) good and evil fruits; thyself harmonized by the Yoga of renunciation, thou shalt come unto Me when set free. (28)

[1] Elementals or nature-spirits.

The same am I to all beings; there is none hateful to Me nor dear. They verily who worship Me with devotion, they are in Me, and I also in them. (29)

Even if the most sinful worship Me, with undivided heart, he too must be accounted righteous, for he hath rightly resolved; (30)

Speedily he becometh dutiful and goeth to eternal peace. O Kaunteya, know thou for certain that My devotee perisheth never. (31)

They who take refuge with Me, O Pârtha! though of the womb of sin, women, Vaishyas, even Shûdras, they also tread the highest Path. (32)

How much rather then holy Brâhmanas and devoted royal saints; having obtained this transient joyless world, worship thou Me. (33)

On Me (fix) thy Manas; be devoted to Me; sacrifice to Me; prostrate thyself before Me; harmonised thus in the SELF, thou shalt come unto Me, having Me as thy supreme goal.

Thus in the glorious Upanishads of the BHAGAVAD GÎTÂ, the science of Brahman, the scripture of Yoga, the dialogue between Shrî Krishna and Arjuna, the ninth discourse, entitled:

THE YOGA OF THE KINGLY SCIENCE AND THE KINGLY SECRET.

TENTH DISCOURSE.

The Blessed Lord said:

Again, O mighty-armed, hear thou My supreme word, that desiring thy welfare, I will declare to thee who art belòved. (1)

The multitude of the Gods, or the great Rishis, know not My forthcoming, for I am the beginning of all the Gods and the great Rishis. (2)

He who knoweth Me, unborn, beginningless, the great Lord of the world, he among mortals without delusion, is liberated from all sin. (3)

Buddhi, wisdom, non-illusion, forgiveness, truth, self-restraint, calmness, pleasure, pain, existence, non-existence, fear and also courage, (4)

Harmlessness, equanimity, content, austerity, almsgiving, fame and obloquy, are the various characteristics of beings issuing from Me. (5)

The seven great Rishis, the ancient Four, and also the Manus, were born of My nature and mind; of them this race was generated. (6)

He who knows in essence that sovereignty and Yoga of Mine, he is harmonised by unfaltering Yoga; there is no doubt thereof. (7)

I am the Generator of all; all evolves from Me; understanding thus, the wise adore Me, in rapt devotion. (8)

Mindful of Me, their life hidden in Me, illumining each other, ever conversing about Me, they are content and joyful. (9)

To these, ever harmonious, worshipping in love, I give the Buddhi-Yoga by which they come unto Me. (10)

Out of pure compassion for them,

dwelling within their SELF, I destroy the ignorance-born darkness by the shining lamp of wisdom. (11)

Arjuna said:

"Thou art the supreme Brahman, the supreme Abode, the supreme Purity; Purusha, eternal, divine, primeval God, unborn, the Lord!" (12)

All the Rishis have thus acclaimed Thee, as also the divine Rishi, Nârada; so Asita, Devala, and Vyâsa; and now Thou Thyself tellest it me. (13)

All this I believe true that Thou sayest to me, O Keshava. Thy manifestation, O Blessed Lord, neither Gods nor Dânavas comprehend. (14)

Thyself indeed knowest Thyself by Thyself, O Purushottama! Source of beings, Lord of beings, God of Gods, Ruler of the world! (15)

Deign to tell without reserve of Thy divine self-sovereignty, by which sovereignty Thou stayest, pervading these worlds. (16)

How may I know Thee, O Yogî, by constant meditation? In what, in what aspects art Thou to be thought of by me, O blessed Lord? (17)

In detail tell me again of Thy Yoga and sovereignty, O Janârdana; there is for me never satiety in hearing Thy life-giving words. (18)

The Blessed Lord said:

Blessed be thou! I will declare to thee My divine sovereignty by its chief characteristics, O best of the Kurus; there is no end to details of Me. (19)

I, O Gudâkesha, am the SELF, seated in the heart of all beings; I am the beginning, the middle, and also the end of all beings. (20)

Of the Âdityas I am Vishnu; of radiances the glorious sun; I am Marîchi of the Maruts, of the asterisms the moon am I. (21)

Of the Vedas I am the Sâma-Veda, I am Vâsava of the Gods; and of the senses I am Manas, I am of living beings the intelligence. (22)

And of the Rudras Shankara am I, Vittesha of the Yakshas and Râkshasas;[1] and of the Vasus I am Pâvaka, Meru of high mountains am I. (23)

And know Me, O Pârtha, of household priests the chief, Vrihaspati; of generals I am Skanda, of lakes I am the ocean. (24)

Of the great Rishis Bhrigu, of speech I am the one syllable;[2] of sacrifices I am the sacrifice of silent repetitions,[3] of immovable things the Himâlaya. (25)

Asvattha of all trees, and of divine Rishis Nârada; of Gandharvas Chitra-

[1] Yakshas are demigods: Râkshasas powerful and energetic demons.

[2] Om. [3] Japa.

ratha, of the perfected the Muni Kapila. (26)

Uchchaishravas of horses know Me, Amrita-born; Airâvata of lordly elephants, and of men the monarch. (27)

Of weapons I am the thunderbolt, of cows I am Kâmaduk: I am Kandarpa of the progenitors, of serpents Vâsuki am I. (28)

And I am Ananta of Nâgas, Varuna of sea-dwellers I; and of Pitris Aryaman, Yama of governors am I. (29)

And I am Prahlâda of Daityas, of measures time am I; and of wild beasts I the imperial beast,[1] and Vainateya of birds. (30)

Of purifiers I am the wind, Râma of warriors I; and I am Makara of fishes, of streams the Ganga am I. (31)

Of creations the beginning and the ending, and also the middle am I, O Arjuna. Of sciences the science of

[1] Lion.

Adhyâtmâ, the right argument of orators I. (32)

Of letters the letter A I am, and the Dvandva of a compound; I also inexhaustible time, I the supporter whose face turns everywhere. (33)

And all-devouring death am I, and the origin of all to come: and of feminine qualities honour, prosperity, speech, memory, intelligence, constancy, forgiveness. (34)

Of hymns also Vrihatsâman, Gâyatrî of metres am I; of months I am Mârgashîrsha, of seasons the flowery. (35)

I am the gambling of the cheat, and the splendour of splendid things I; I am victory, I am determination, and the truth of the truthful I. (36)

Of the Vrîshnis Vâsudeva am I, of the Pândavas Dhananjaya; of the Munis also I am Vyâsa, of wise men Ushana the Sage. (37)

Of rulers I am the sceptre, of those

that seek victory I am statesmanship; and of secrets I am also silence, the knowledge of knowers am I. (38)

And whatsoever is the seed of all beings, that am I, O Arjuna! nor is there aught, moving or unmoving, that may exist bereft of Me. (39)

There is no end of My divine powers, O Parantapa! What has been declared is illustrative of My infinite sovereignty. (40)

Whatsoever is royal, good, beautiful, and mighty, understand thou that to go forth from My splendour. (41)

But what is the knowledge of all these details to thee, O Arjuna? Having pervaded this whole universe with a portion of Myself, I remain. (42)

Thus in the glorious Upanishads of the BHAGAVAD GÎTÂ, the science of Brahman, the scripture of Yoga, the dialogue between Shrî Krishna and Arjuna, the tenth discourse, entitled:

THE YOGA OF SOVEREIGNTY.

ELEVENTH DISCOURSE.

Arjuna said:

This word of the Supreme Secret, named Adhyâtma, Thou hast spoken out of compassion; by this my delusion is taken away. (1)

The production and destruction of beings have been heard by me in detail from Thee, O Lotus-eyed, and also Thy imperishable greatness. (2)

Even as Thou describest Thyself, O supreme Îshvara,[1] I desire to see Thy form omnipotent, O best of beings. (3)

If thou thinkest that by me It can be seen, O Lord, Lord of Yoga, then show me Thine imperishable SELF. (4)

[1] The supreme Lord as creator and ruler of a universe.

The Blessed Lord said:

Behold, O Pârtha, the form of Me, a hundredfold, a thousandfold, various in kind, divine, various in colour and shape. (5)

Behold the Âdityas, the Vasus, the Rudras, the two Ashvins and also the Maruts; behold many marvels never seen ere this, O Bhârata. (6)

Here, to-day, behold the whole universe, movable and immovable, standing in one, in My body, O Gudâkesha, with aught else thou desirest to see. (7)

But verily thou art not able to behold Me with these thine eyes; the divine eye I give unto thee! Behold My sovereign Yoga! (8)

Sanjaya said:

Having thus spoken, O King, the great Lord of Yoga, Hari, showed to

Pârtha his supreme form as Îshvara. (9)

With many mouths and eyes, with many visions of marvel, with many divine ornaments, with many upraised divine weapons; (10)

Wearing divine necklaces and vestures, anointed with divine unguents, the God all marvellous, boundless, with face turned everywhere. (11)

If the splendour of a thousand suns were to blaze out together in the sky, that might resemble the glory of that Mahâtmâ. (12)

There Pândava beheld the whole universe, divided into manifold parts, standing in one, in the body of the God of Gods. (13)

Then he, Dhananjaya, overwhelmed with astonishment, his hair upstanding with delight, bowed down his head to the God, and with joined palms spake. (14)

Arjuna said:

Within Thy form, O God, the Gods I see,
All grades of beings with distinctive marks;
Brahmâ, the Lord, upon His lotus-thorne,
The Rishi all and Serpents, the Divine. (15)

With mouths, eyes, arms, breasts,[1] multitudinous,
I see Thee everywhere, unbounded Form.
Beginning, middle, end, nor source of Thee,
Infinite Lord, infinite Form, I find; (16)

Shining, a mass of splendour everywhere,
With discus, mace, tiara, I behold:
Blazing as fire, as sun, dazzling the gaze

[1] Literally, stomach.

From all sides in the sky, immeasurable. (17)
Lofty beyond all thought, unperishing,
Thou treasure-house supreme; all-immanent,
Eternal Dharma's changeless Guardian, Thou;
As immemorial Man I think of Thee. (18)
Nor source, nor midst nor ènd! infinite force,
Unnumbered arms, the sun and moon Thine eyes!
I see Thy face, as sacrificial fire
Blazing, its splendour burneth up the worlds. (19)
By Thee alone are filled the earth, the heavens,
And all the regions that are stretched between;
The triple worlds sink down, O mighty One,

Before Thine awful manifested Form. (20)

To Thee the troops of Suras enter in,
Some with joined palms in awe invoking Thee;
Banded Maharshis, Siddhas, "Svasti!" cry,
Chanting Thy praises with resounding songs. (21)

Rudras, Vasus, Sâdhyas and Âdityas,
Vishvas, the Ashvins, Maruts, Ushmapas,
Gandharvas, Yakshas, Siddhas, Asuras.
In wondering multitudes beholding Thee. (22)

Thy mighty Form, with many mouths and eyes,
Long-armed, with thighs and feet innumerate,
Vast-bosomed, set with many fearful teeth,
The worlds see terror-struck, as also I. (23)

Radiant Thou touchest heaven; rain-
bow-hued,
With opened mouths and shining vast-
orbed eyes.
My inmost self is quaking, having
seen,
My strength is withered, Vishnu, and
my peace. (24)
Like Time's destroying flames I see
Thy teeth,
Upstanding, spread within expanded
jaws;
Nought know I anywhere, no shelter
find,
Mercy, O God! refuge of all the worlds!
(25)
The sons of Dhritarâshtra, and with
them
The multitude of all these kings of
earth,
Bhîshma, Drona, Sûta's royal son,
And all the noblest warriors of our
hosts, (26)

Into Thy gaping mouths they hurrying rush,
Tremendous-toothed and terrible to see;
Some caught within the gaps between Thy teeth
Are seen, their heads to powder crushed and ground. (27)
As river-floods impetuously rush,
Hurling their waters into ocean's lap,
So fling themselves into Thy flaming mouths,
In haste, these mighty men, these lords of earth. (28)
As moths with quickened speed will headlong fly
Into a flaming light, to fall destroyed,
So also these, in haste precipitate,
Enter within Thy mouths destroyed to fall. (29)
On every side, all-swallowing, fiery-tongued,
Thou lickest up mankind, devouring all;
Thy glory filleth space: the universe

Is burning, Vishnu, with Thy blazing
 rays. (30)
Reveal Thy SELF; what awful Form
 art Thou?
I worship Thee! Have mercy, God
 supreme!
Thine inner being I am fain to
 know;
This Thy forthstreaming Life bewild-
 ers me. (31)

The Blessed Lord said:

Time am I, laying desolate the world,
Made manifest on earth to slay man-
 kind!
Not one of all these warriors ranged for
 strife
Escapeth death; thou shalt alone sur-
 vive. (32)
Therefore stand up! win for thyself re-
 nown,
Conquer thy foes, enjoy the spacious
 realm.
By Me they are already overcome,

Be thou the outward cause, left-handed
one. (33)
Drona and Bhîshma and Jayadratha,
Karna and all the other warriors here
Are slain by Me. Destroy then fearlessly,
Fight! thou shalt crush thy rivals in the field. (34)

Sanjaya said:

Having heard these words of Keshava, he who weareth a diadem, with joined palms, quaking, and prostrating himself, spake again to Krishna, stammering with fear, casting down his face. (35)

Arjuna said:

Hrishîkesha! in Thy magnificence
Rightly the world rejoiceth, bound to Thee;
The Râkshasas to every quarter fly
In fear; the hosts of Siddhas prostrate fall. (36)

How should they otherwise, O loftiest
SELF!
First Cause! Brahmâ Himself less great
than Thou.
Infinite, God of Gods, home of all
worlds,
Unperishing, Sat Asat, THAT supreme!
(37)
First of the Gods, most ancient Man
Thou art,
Supreme receptacle of all that lives,
Knower and known, the dwelling-place
on high,
In Thy vast Form the universe is
spread. (38)
Thou art Vâyu and Yama, Agni, moon,
Varuna, Father, Grandsire of all:
Hail, hail to Thee! a thousand times
all hail!
Hail unto Thee! again, again, all hail!
(39)
Prostrate in front of Thee, prostrate
behind,

Prostrate on every side to Thee, O All.
In power boundless, measureless in strength,
Thou holdest all: then Thou Thyself art All. (40)
If, thinking Thee but friend, importunate,
O Krishna! or O Yâdava! O friend!
I cried, unknowing of Thy majesty,
And careless in the fondness of my love; (41)
If jesting, I irreverence showed to Thee,
At play, reposing, sitting or at meals,
Alone, O sinless One, or with my friends,
Forgive my error, O Thou boundless One. (42)
Father of worlds, of all that moves and stands,
Worthier of reverence than the Guru's self,
There is none like to Thee. Who passeth Thee?

Pre-eminent Thy power in all the
worlds. (43)
Therefore I fall before Thee; with my
body
I worship as is fitting; bless Thou
me.
As father with the son, as friend with
friend,
With the beloved as lover, bear with
me. (44)
I have seen That which none hath seen
before,
My heart is glad, yet faileth me for
fear;
Show me, O God, Thine other Form
again,
Mercy, O God of Gods, home of all
worlds. (45)
Diademed, mace and discus in Thy
hand,
Again I fain would see Thee as before;
Put on again Thy four-armed shape, O
Lord,

O thousand-armed, of forms innumer-
ate. (46)

The Blessed Lord said:

Arjuna, by My favour thou hast seen
This loftiest form by Yoga's self re-
vealed!
Radiant, all-penetrating, endless, first,
That none except thyself hath ever
seen. (47)
Nor sacrifice nor Vedas, alms nor works,
Nor sharp austerity, nor study deep,
Can win the vision of this Form for man.
Foremost of Kurus, thou alone hast
seen. (48)
Be not bewildered, be thou not afraid,
Because thou hast beheld this awful
Form;
Cast fear away, and let thy heart rejoice;
Behold again Mine own familiar shape.
(49)

Sanjaya said:

Vâsudeva, having thus spoken to Arjuna, again manifested His own Form, and consoled the terrified one, the Mahâtmâ again assuming a gentle form. (50)

Arjuna said:

Beholding again Thy gentle human Form, O Janârdana, I am now collected, and am restored to my own nature. (51)

The Blessed Lord said:

This Form of Mine beholden by thee is very hard to see. Verily the Gods ever long to behold this Form.

Nor can I be seen as thou hast seen Me by the Vedas, nor by austerities, nor by alms, or by offerings; (53)

But by devotion to Me alone I may thus be perceived, Arjuna, and known and seen in essence, and entered O Parantapa. (54)

He who doeth actions for Me, whose supreme good I am, My devotee, freed from attachment, without hatred of any being, he cometh unto Me, O Pândava.

(55)

Thus in the glorious Upanishads of the Bhagavad Gîtâ, the science of Brahman, the scripture of Yoga, the dialogue between Shri Krishna and Arjunâ, the eleventh discourse, entitled:

THE YOGA OF THE VISION OF THE UNIVERSAL FORM.

TWELFTH DISCOURSE.

Arjuna said:

Those devotees who ever harmonised worship Thee, and those also (who worship) the Indestructible, the Unmanifested, whether of these is the more learned in Yoga? (1)

The Blessed Lord said:

They who with Manas fixed on Me, ever harmonised worship Me, with faith supreme endowed, these in My opinion, are best in Yoga. (2)

They who worship the Indestructible, the Ineffable, the Unmanifested, Omnipresent and Unthinkable, the Unchanging, Immutable, Eternal, (3)

Renouncing and subduing the senses, regarding everything equally, in the welfare of all rejoicing, these also come unto Me. (4)

The difficulty of those whose minds are set on the Unmanifested is greater; for the path of the Unmanifested is hard for the embodied to reach. (5)

Those verily who, renouncing all actions in Me, and intent on Me, worship meditating on Me, with whole-hearted Yoga, (6)

These I speedily lift up from the ocean of death and existence, O Pârtha, their minds being fixed on Me. (7)

Place thy Manas in Me, into Me let thy Buddhi enter; then without doubt thou shalt abide in Me hereafter. (8)

But if thou are not able firmly to fix thy mind on Me, then by the Yoga of practice seek to reach Me, O Dhananjaya. (9)

If also thou art not equal to constant practice, be intent on my service; performing actions for my sake, thou shalt attain perfection. (10)

If to do this even thou hast not strength, then taking refuge in union with Me renounce then all fruit of action, with the self controlled. (11)

Better indeed is wisdom than constant practice; than wisdom meditation is better: than meditation renunciation of the fruit of action; on renunciation follows peace. (12)

He who beareth no ill-will to any being, friendly and compassionate, without attachment and egoism, balanced in pleasure and pain, and forgiving, (13)

Ever-content, harmonious, with the self controlled, resolute, with Manas and Buddhi dedicated to Me, he, My devotee, is dear to Me. (14)

He from whom the world doth not

shrink away, who doth not shrink away from the world, freed from the anxieties of joy, anger and fear, he is dear to Me. (15)

He who wants nothing, is pure, expert, passionless, untroubled, renouncing every undertaking, he, My devotee, is dear to Me. (16)

He who neither loveth nor hateth, nor grieveth, nor desireth, renouncing good and evil, full of devotion, he is dear to Me. (17)

Alike to foe and friend, and also in fame and ignominy, alike in cold and heat, pleasures and pains, destitute of attachment, (18)

Taking equally praise and reproach, silent, wholly content with what cometh, homeless, firm in mind, full of devotion, that man is dear to Me. (19)

They verily who partake of this Amrita-Dharma, as taught herein, endued with faith, I their supreme (Object), devotees, they are surpassingly dear to Me. (20)

Thus in the glorious Upanishads of the BHAGAVAD GÎTÂ, the science of Brahman, the scripture of Yoga, the dialogue between Shri Krishna and Arjuna, the twelfth discourse, entitled:

THE YOGA OF DEVOTION.

THIRTEENTH DISCOURSE.

The Blessed Lord said:

This body, son of Kuntî, is called the Field; that which knoweth it is called the Knower of the Field by the Sages. (1)

Understand Me as the Knower of the Field in all Fields, O Bhârata. Wisdom as to the Field and the Knower of the Field, that in My opinion is the wisdom. (2)

What that Field is and of what nature, how modified, and whence it is, and what He[1] is and what His powers, hear that now briefly from Me. (3)

Rishis have sung in manifold ways, in many various chants, and in decisive Brahma-sûtra verses, full of reasonings. (4)

[1] Kshetragnya, the Knower of the Field.

The great elements, Ahankâra, Buddhi and also the Unmanifested, the ten senses, and the one, and the five pastures of the senses; (5)

Desire, aversion, pleasure, pain, combination,[1] intelligence, firmness, these, briefly described, constitute the Field and its modifications. (6)

Humility, unpretentiousness, harmlessness, forgiveness, rectitude, service of the teacher, purity, steadfastness, self-control, (7)

Indifference to the objects of the senses, and also absence of egoism, insight into the pain and evil of birth, death, old age and sickness, (8)

Unattachment, absence of self-identification with son, wife or home, and constant balance of mind in wished-for and unwished-for events, (9)

Unflinching devotion to Me, without union with another, resort to seques-

[1] The body.

tered places, absence of enjoyment in the company of men, (10)

Constancy in the Adhyâtmâ-wisdom, understanding of the object of essential wisdom; that is declared to be wisdom; all against it is ignorance. (11)

I will declare that which is to be known, that which being known immortality is enjoyed—the beginningless supreme Brahman, called neither being nor non-being. (12)

Everywhere THAT has hands and feet, everywhere eyes, heads, and mouths; all-hearing, He dwelleth in the world, enveloping all. (13)

Shining with all sense-faculties without any senses; unattached supporting everything; and free from attributes enjoying attributes. (14)

Without and within all beings, immovable and also movable; by reason of His subtlety imperceptible; at hand and far away is THAT. (15)

Not divided amid beings, and yet seated distributively; THAT is to be known as the supporter of beings; He devours and He generates. (16)

THAT, the Light of all lights, is said to be beyond darkness; wisdom, the object of wisdom, the end of wisdom, seated in the hearts of all.

Thus the Field, wisdom and the object of wisdom, have been briefly told. My devotee, thus knowing, enters into My Being. (18)

Know thou that Prakriti and Purusha are both without beginning; and know thou also that modifications and attributes are all Prakriti-born. (19)

Prakriti is called the cause of the generation of causes and effects; Purusha is called the cause of the enjoyment of pleasure and pain. (20)

Purusha seated in Prakriti useth the attributes born of Prakriti; the attachment to the attributes is the cause of his births in good and evil wombs. (21)

Spectator and permitter, supporter, enjoyer, the great Îshvara, and also the supreme SELF; thus is styled in this body the supreme Purusha. (22)

He who thus knoweth the Purusha and the Prakriti with its attributes, in whatsoever condition he may be, he shall not be born again. (23)

Some by meditation behold the SELF in the self by the SELF; others by the Sânkhya Yoga, and others by the Yoga of action; (24)

Others also, ignorant of this, having heard of it from others, worship; and these also cross beyond death, adhering to what they had heard. (25)

Whatsoever creature is born, immobile or mobile, know thou, O best of the Bhâratas, it is from the union between the Field and the Knower of the Field. (26)

Seated equally in all beings, the supreme Îshvara, indestructible within the destructible—he who thus seeth, he seeth. (27)

Seeing indeed everywhere the same, Îshvara equally dwelling, he doth not destroy the SELF by the self, and thus reacheth the supreme Goal. (28)

He who seeth that Prakriti verily performeth all actions, and that the SELF is actionless, he seeth. (29)

When he perceiveth the diversified existence of beings as rooted in One, and proceeding from it, then he reacheth Brahman. (30)

Being beginningless and without attributes, the imperishable supreme SELF, though seated in the body, O Kaunteya, worketh not nor is affected. (31)

As the omnipresent Âkâsha is not affected, by reason of its subtlety, so seated everywhere in the body the SELF is not affected. (32)

As the one sun illumineth the whole earth, so the Lord of the Field illumineth the whole Field, O Bhârata. (33)

They who by the eye of wisdom perceive this difference between the Field and the Knower of the Field, and the liberation of beings from Prakriti, they go to the Supreme. (34)

Thus in the glorious Upanishads of the BHAGAVAD GÎTÂ, the science of Brahman, the scripture of Yoga, the dialogue between Shrî Krishna and Arjuna, the thirteenth discourse, entitled:

THE YOGA OF THE DISTINCTION BETWEEN THE FIELD AND THE KNOWER OF THE FIELD.

FOURTEENTH DISCOURSE.

The Blessed Lord said:

I will again proclaim that supreme wisdom, of all wisdom the best, which all the Munis having known have gone hence to the supreme Perfection. (1)

Having taken refuge in this wisdom and being assimilated to My own nature, they are not re-born even in the emanation of a universe, nor are disquieted in the dissolution. (2)

My womb is the Mahat-Brahma; in that I place the germ; thence cometh the production of all beings, O Bhârata. (3)

In whatsoever wombs mortals are produced, O Kaunteya, the Mahat-Brahma is their womb, I their generating father.

(4)

Sattva, Rajas, Tamas, such are the Gunas, Prakriti-born; they bind fast in the body, O great-armed one, the indestructible dweller in the body. (5)

Of these Sattva, from its stainlessness luminous and healthy, bindeth by the attachment to bliss and the attachment to wisdom, O sinless one. (6)

Rajas, the passion-nature, know thou, is the source of attachment and thirst for life, O Kaunteya, that bindeth the dweller in the body by the attachment to action. (7)

But Tamas, know thou, born of unwisdom, is the deluder of all dwellers in the body; that bindeth by heedlessness, indolence and sloth, O Bhârata. (8)

Sattva attacheth to bliss, Rajas to action, O Bhârata. Tamas, verily having shrouded wisdom, attacheth on the contrary to heedlessness. (9)

Now Sattva prevaileth, overcoming

Rajas and Tamas, O Bhârata. (Now) Rajas (overcoming) Sattva and Tamas; and (now) Tamas (overcoming) Sattva and Rajas. (10)

When the wisdom-light streameth forth from all the gates of the body, then it may be known that Sattva is increasing. (11)

Greed, outgoing energy, undertaking of actions, restlessness, desire—these are born of the increase of Rajas, O best of the Bhâratas. (12)

Darkness, stagnation and heedlessness and also delusion—these are born of the increase of Tamas, O joy of the Kurus. (13)

If Sattva verily prevaileth when the embodied goeth to dissolution, then he goeth forth to the spotless words of the great sages. (14)

Having gone to dissolution in Rajas, he is born among those attached to action; if dissolved in Tamas, he is born in the wombs of the senseless. (15)

It is said the fruit of a good action is Sâttvic and spotless; verily the fruit of Rajas is pain, and the fruit of Tamas unwisdom. (16)

From Sattva wisdom is born, and also greed from Rajas; heedlessness and delusion are of Tamas and also unwisdom. (17)

They rise upwards who are settled in Sattva; the Râjasic dwell in the midmost place; the Tâmasic go downwards, enveloped in the vilest qualities. (18)

When the Seer perceiveth no agent other than the Gunas, and knoweth THAT which is higher than the Gunas, he entereth into My nature. (19)

When the dweller in the body hath crossed over these three Gunas, whence all bodies have been produced, liberated from birth, death, old age and sorrow, he drinketh the nectar of immortality.[1] (20)

Arjuna said:

What are the marks of him who hath crossed over the three Gunas, O Lord? How acteth he, and how doth he go beyond these three Gunas? (21)

The Blessed Lord said:

He, O Pândava, who hateth not radiance, nor outgoing energy, nor even delusion when present, nor longeth after them, absent; (22)

He who, seated as a neutral, is unshaken by the Gunas; who saying, "The Gunas revolve;" standeth apart, immovable, (23)

Balanced in pleasure and pain, self-reliant, to whom a lump of earth, a rock and gold are alike; the same to loved and unloved, firm, the same in censure and in praise, (24)

The same in honour and ignominy,

[1] The Amrita.

the same to friend and foe, abandoning all undertakings—he is said to have crossed over the Gunas. (25)

And he who serveth Me exclusively by the Yoga of devotion, he, crossing beyond the Gunas, he is fit to become Brahman. (26)

For I am the abode of Brahman, and of the indestructible nectar of immortality, of immemorial Dharma, and of unending bliss. (27)

Thus in the glorious Upanishads of the BHAGAVAD GÎTÂ, the science of Brahman, the scripture of Yoga, the dialogue between Shrî Krishna and Arjuna, the fourteenth discourse, entitled:

THE YOGA OF SEPARATION FROM THE THREE GUNAS.

FIFTEENTH DISCOURSE.

The Blessed Lord said:

With roots above, branches below, the Asvattha is said to be indestructible; the leaves of it are hymns; he who knoweth it is a Veda-knower. (1)

Downwards and upwards spread the branches of it, nourished by the Gunas, the objects of the senses its buds; and its roots grow downwards, the bonds of action in the world of men. (2)

Nor here may be acquired knowledge of its form, nor its end, nor its origin, nor its rooting-place; this strongly-rooted Asvattha having been cut down by the unswerving weapon of non-attachment, (3)

That path beyond may be sought, treading which there is no return. I go indeed to that original Purusha whence the ancient energy forth-streamed. (4)

Without pride and delusion, victorious over the vice of attachment, dwelling constantly in Âtmâ, desire pacified, liberated from the pairs of opposites known as pleasure and pain, they tread, undeluded, that indestructible path. (5)

Nor doth the sun lighten there, nor moon, nor fire; having gone whither they return not; that is My supreme dwelling-place. (6)

A portion of Mine own Self, transformed in the world of life into an immortal Gîva,[1] draweth round itself the senses of which Manas is the sixth, placed in Prakriti. (7)

[1] A living soul, individualized from the Universal Spirit.

10

When the Lord acquireth a body and when He abandoneth it, He seizeth these and goeth with them, as the wind (takes) fragrances from their retreats. (8)

Enshrined in the ear, the eye, the touch, the taste and the smell, and in Manas also, He enjoyeth the objects of the senses. (9)

The deluded do not perceive Him when He departeth or stayeth, or enjoyeth, swayed by the Gunas; the wisdom-eyed perceive. (10)

Yogîs also, struggling, perceive Him, established in the SELF; but though struggling, the unintelligent perceive Him not, their self untrained. (11)

That splendour issuing from the sun that enlighteneth the whole world, that which is in the moon and in fire, that splendour know as from Me. (12)

Permeating the soil, I support beings by My vital energy, and having become the delicious Soma[1] I nourish all plants. (13)

I, having become Vaishvânara, take possession of the bodies of breathing things, and united with Prâna and Apâna, I digest the four kinds of food. (14)

And I am seated in the hearts of all, and from Me memory and wisdom and their absence. And that which is to be known in all the Vedas am I; and I indeed the Veda-knower and the author of the Vedânta. (15)

There are two Purushas in this world, the destructible and the indestructible; the destructible (is) all beings, the unchanging (is) called the indestructible. (16)

The highest Purusha is verily Another, declared as the supreme SELF.

[1] "Having become the watery moon" is the accepted translation.

He who pervading sustaineth the three worlds, the indestructible Îshvara. (17)

Since I excel the destructible, and am more excellent also than the indestructible, in the world and in the Veda I am proclaimed Purushottama.[1] (18)

He who undeluded knoweth Me thus as Purushottama, he, all-knowing, worshippeth Me with his whole being, O Bhârata. (19)

Thus by Me this most secret teaching hath been told, O sinless one. This known, he hath become illuminated, and hath finished his work, O Bhârata. (20)

Thus in the glorious Upanishads of the BHAGAVAD GÎTÂ, the science of Brahman, the scripture of Yoga, the dialogue between Shrî Krishna and Arjuna, the fifteenth discourse, entitled:

THE YOGA OF ATTAINING PURUSHOTTAMA.

[1] The highest Purusha.

SIXTEENTH DISCOURSE.

Fearlessness, cleanness of life, steadfastness in the Yoga of wisdom, almsgiving, self-restraint and sacrifice and study of the Shâstras, austerity and straightforwardness, (1)

Harmlessness, truth, absence of wrath, renunciation, peacefulness, absence of crookedness, compassion to living beings, uncovetousness, mildness, modesty, absence of fickleness, (2)

Vigour, forgiveness, fortitude, purity, absence of envy and pride—these are his who is born with the divine properties, O Bhârata. (3)

Hypocrisy, arrogance and conceit, wrath and also harshness and unwisdom are his who is born, O Pârtha, with âsuric[1] properties. (4)

[1] The Asuras were the enemies of the Suras, or gods; "demoniac properties" might be said.

The divine properties are deemed (to be) for liberation, the âsuric for bondage. Grieve not, thou art born with divine properties, O Pândava. (5)

Twofold is the animal creation in this world, the divine and the âsuric; the divine hath been described at length; hear from Me, O Pârtha, the âsuric. (6)

Âsuric men know not either right energy or right abstinence; nor purity, nor even propriety, nor truth is in them (7)

"The universe is without truth, without (moral) basis," they say, "without a God,[1] brought about by mutual union and caused by lust and nothing else." (8)

Holding this view, these ruined selves of small Buddhi, of fierce deeds, come forth as enemies for the destruction of the world. (9)

Surrendering themselves to insatiable desires, possessed with vanity, concei

[1] Îshvara, the ruler of a universe.

and arrogance, holding evil ideas through delusion, (they) engage in action with impure resolves. (10)

Giving themselves over to unmeasured thought whose end is death, regarding the gratification of desires as the highest, feeling sure that this is all, (11)

Held in bondage by a hundred ties of expectation, given over to lust and anger, they strive to obtain by unlawful means hoards of wealth for sensual enjoyments. (12)

"This to-day by me hath been won, that purpose I shall gain; this wealth is mine already, and also this shall be mine in future. (13)

"I have slain this enemy, and others also I shall slay. I am the Lord, I am the enjoyer, I am perfect, powerful, happy; (14)

"I am wealthy, well-born; what other is there that is like unto me? I will sacrifice, I will give (alms), I will rejoice." Thus deluded by unwisdom, (15)

Bewildered by numerous thoughts, enmeshed in the web of delusion, addicted to the gratification of desire, they fall downwards into a foul hell. (16)

Self-sufficing, obstinate, filled with the pride and intoxication of wealth, they perform lip-sacrifices for ostentation, contrary to scriptural ordinance. (17)

Given over to egoism, power, insolence, lust and wrath, these malicious ones hate Me in the bodies of others and in their own. (18)

These haters, evil, pitiless, vilest among men in the world, I ever throw down into âsuric wombs. (19)

Cast into an âsuric womb, deluded birth after birth, attaining not to Me, O Kaunteya, they sink into the lowest depths. (20

Triple is the gate of this hell, de

structive of the self—lust, wrath and greed; therefore let man renounce these three. (21)

A man liberated from these three gates of darkness, O son of Kuntî, accomplisheth his own welfare and thus reacheth the highest goal. (22)

He who having cast aside the ordinances of the Shâstras, followeth the promptings of desire, attaineth not to perfection, nor happiness, nor the highest goal. (23)

Therefore let the Shâstras be thy authority, in determining what ought to be done, or what ought not to be done. Knowing what hath been declared by the ordinances of the Shâstras, thou oughtest to work in this world. (24)

Thus in the glorious Upanishads of the BHAGAVAD GÎTÂ, the science of Brahman, the scripture of Yoga, the dialogue between Shrî Krishna and Arjuna, the sixteenth discourse, entitled:

THE YOGA OF DIVISION BETWEEN THE DIVINE AND THE ASURIC.

SEVENTEENTH DISCOURSE.

Arjuna said:

Those that sacrifice full of faith,[1] but casting aside the ordinances of the Shâstras, what is verily their condition, O Krishna? (Is it one of) Sattva, Rajas or Tamas? (1)

The Blessed Lord said:

Threefold is by nature the unborn faith of the embodied—sâttvic, râjasic and tâmasic. Hear thou of these. (2)

The faith of each is shaped to his own nature, O Bhârata. The man consists of his faith;[2] that which his faith is, he is even that. (3)

[1] Shraddhâ.

[2] That is, the man's faith shows what is the man's character.

Sâttvic men worship the gods; râjasic the Yakshas and Râkshasas; the others, the tâmasic folk, worship Pretas and troops of Bhûtas.[1] (4)

The men who perform severe austerities, unenjoined by the Shâstras, wedded to vanity and egoism, impelled by the force of their desires and passions, (5)

Unintelligent, tormenting the aggregated elements forming the body, and Me also, seated in the inner body, know these âsuric in their resolves. (6)

The food also which is dear to each is threefold, as also sacrifice, austerity and almsgiving. Hear thou the distinction of these. (7)

The foods that augment vitality, energy, vigour, health, joy and cheerfulness, delicious, bland, substantial and agreeable, are dear to the Sâttvic. (8)

[1] Pretas are ghosts, the departed, while Bhûtas are nature-spirits of a somewhat goblin-like type.

The Râjasic desire foods that are bitter, sour, saline, over-hot, pungent, dry and burning, and which produce pain, grief and sickness. (9)

That which is stale and flat, putrid and corrupt, leavings also and unclean, is the food dear to the Tâmasic. (10)

The sacrifice which is offered by men without desire for fruit, as enjoined by the ordinances, under the firm belief that sacrifice is a duty, that is sâttvic. (11)

The sacrifice offered with a view verily to fruit, and also indeed for self-glorification, O best of the Bhâratas; know thou that to be râjasic. (12)

The sacrifice contrary to the ordinances, without distributing food, devoid of the Mantras and without gifts,[1] empty of faith, is said to be tâmasic. (13)

Worship given to the Gods, to the

[1] To the officiating priests.

twice-born, to Gurus and to the wise, purity, straightforwardness, continence and harmlessness, are called the austerity of the body. (14)

Speech causing no annoyance, truthful, pleasant and beneficial, the practice of the study of the Shâstras, are called the austerity of speech. (15)

Mental happiness, equilibrium, silence, self-control, purity of nature—this is called the austerity of the mind.[1] (16)

This threefold austerity, performed by men with the utmost faith, without desire for fruit, harmonised, is said to be sâttvic. (17)

The austerity which is practised with the object of gaining respect, honour and reverence, and for ostentation, is said to be râjasic, unstable and fleeting. (18)

That austerity done under a deluded understanding, with self-torture, or

[1] Manas.

with the object of destroying another, that is declared tâmasic. (19)

That alms given to one who does nothing in return, believing that a gift ought to be made, in a (fit) place and time, to a worthy person, that alms is accounted sâttvic. (20)

That given with a view to receiving in return, or looking for fruit again, or grudgingly, that alms is accounted râjasic. (21)

That alms given at unfit place and time, and to unworthy persons, disrespectfully and contemptuously, that is declared tâmasic. (22)

"OM TAT SAT," this has been considered to be the threefold designation of Brahman. By that were ordained of old Brâhmans, Vedas and sacrifices. (23)

Therefore with the pronunciation of "OM" the acts of sacrifice, gift and austerity as laid down in the order nances are always commenced by the knowers of Brahman. (24)

With the pronunciation of "TAT" and without aiming at fruit are performed the various acts of sacrifice, austerity and gift, by those desiring liberation. (25)

"SAT" is used in the sense of reality and goodness; likewise, O Pârtha, the word "SAT" is used in the sense of a good work. (26)

Steadfastness in sacrifice, austerity and gift is also called "SAT," and an action for the sake of THAT is also named "SAT." (27)

Whatsoever is wrought without faith, oblation, gift, austerity, or other deed, "Asat" it is called, O Pârtha; it is nought, here or hereafter. (28)

Thus in the glorious Upanishads of the BHAGAVAD GÎTÂ, the science of Brahman, the scripture of Yoga, the dialogue between Shrî Krishna and Arjuna, the seventeenth discourse, entitled:

THE YOGA OF THE DIVISION OF THREEFOLD FAITH.

EIGHTEENTH DISCOURSE.

Arjuna said:

I desire, O mighty-armed! to know severally the essence of renunciation,[1] O Hrishîkesha, and of relinquishment,[2] O Keshinisûdana.[3] (1)

The Blessed Lord said:

Sages have known as renunciation the renouncing of works with desire; the relinquishing of the fruit of all actions is called relinquishment by the wise. (2)

"Action should be relinquished as an evil,"[4] declare some thoughtful men;

[1] Sannyâsa.

[2] Tyâga.

[3] Slayer of Keshi, a demon.

[4] Some read: "because it is evil."

"acts of sacrifice, gift and austerity should not be relinquished," say others. (3)

Hear my conclusions as to that relinquishment, O best of the Bhâratas; since relinquishment, O tiger of men, has been explained as threefold. (4)

Acts of sacrifice, gift and austerity should not be relinquished, but should be performed; sacrifice, gift and also austerity are the purifiers of the intelligent. (5)

But even these actions should be done leaving aside attachment and fruit, O Pârtha; that is my certain and best belief. (6)

Verily renunciation of actions that are prescribed is not proper; the relinquishment thereof from delusion is said to be tâmasic. (7)

He who relinquisheth an action from fear of physical suffering, saying, "Painful," (thus) performing a râjasic relinquishment obtaineth not the fruit of relinquishment. (8)

He who performeth a prescribed action, saying, "It ought to be done," O Arjuna, relinquishing attachment and also fruit, that relinquishment is regarded as sâttvic. (9)

The relinquisher pervaded by Sattva, intelligent and with doubts cut away, hateth not unpleasurable action nor is attached to pleasurable. (10)

Nor indeed can embodied beings completely relinquish action; verily he who relinquisheth the fruit of action he is said to be a relinquisher. (11)

Good, evil and mixed—threefold is the fruit of action hereafter for the non-relinquisher; but there is none ever for the renouncer. (12)

These five causes, O mighty-armed, learn of Me as declared in the Sânkhya system for the accomplishment of all actions— (13)

The body, the actor, the various organs, the divers kinds of energies, and the (presiding) deities also, the fifth. (14)

Whatever action a man performeth by his body, speech and mind,[1] whether right or the reverse, these five are the cause thereof. (15)

That being so, he verily who—owing to untrained Buddhi—looketh on his SELF, which is isolated, as the actor, he, of perverted intelligence, seeth not. (16)

He who is free from the egoistic notion, whose Buddhi is not affected, though he slay these peoples, he slayeth not, nor is bound. (17)

Knowledge, the knowable and the knower, the threefold impulse to action; the organ, the action, the actor, the threefold constituents of action. (18)

[1] Manas.

Knowledge, action and actor in the category of gunas are also said to be (severally) threefold, from the difference of gunas; hear thou duly these also. (19)

That by which one indestructible Being is seen in all beings, inseparate in the separated, know thou that knowledge as sâttvic. (20)

But that knowledge which regardeth the several manifold existences in all beings as separate, that knowledge know thou as râjasic. (21)

While that which clingeth to each one thing as if it were the whole, without reason, without grasping the reality, narrow, that is declared to be tâmasic. (22)

An action which is ordained, done by one undesirous of fruit, devoid of attachment, without passion or malice, that is called sâttvic. (23)

But that action that is done by one

longing for desires, or again with egoism, or with much effort, that is declared to be râjasic. (24)

The action undertaken from delusion, without regard to capacity and to consequences—loss and injury (to others)—that is declared to be tâmasic. (25)

Liberated from attachment, not asserting the personality, being an egoist, endued with firmness and vigor, unturned by success or failure, that actor is called sâttvic. (26)

Passionate, desiring to obtain the fruit of actions, greedy, harmful, impure, moved by joy and sorrow, such an actor is pronounced râjasic. (27)

Discordant, vulgar, stubborn, cheating, malicious, indolent, despairful, procrastinating, that actor is called tâmasic. (28)

The division of Buddhi and of firmness also threefold according to the gunas, hear thou related, unreservedly and severally, O Dhananjaya.

That which knoweth energy and abstinence, what ought to be done and what ought not to be done, fear and fearlessness, bondage and liberation, that Buddhi is sâttvic, O Pârtha. (30)

That by which one understandeth awry Dharma and Adharma,[1] and also what ought to be done and what ought not to be done, that Buddhi, O Pârtha, is râjasic. (31)

That which, enwrapped in darkness, thinketh Adharma to be Dharma, and (seeth) all things subverted, that Buddhi, O Pârtha, is tâmasic. (32)

The firmness by which from unwavering Yoga, by which one restraineth the actions of Manas, of the life-breaths and of the sense-organs, that firmness, O Pârtha, is sâttvic. (33).

[1] Right and wrong in the widest sense, law and lawlessness.

But the firmness, O Arjuna, by which, from attachment desirous of fruit, one holdeth fast Dharma, desire and wealth, that firmness, O Pârtha, is râjasic. (34)

That by which one from stupidity doth not abandon sleep, fear, grief, despair, and also vanity, that firmness, O Pârtha, is tâmasic. (35)

And now the threefold kinds of pleasure hear thou from Me, O bull of the Bhâratas; that in which one by practice rejoiceth, and which putteth an end to pain: (36)

Which at first is as venom but in the end is as nectar; that pleasure is said to be sâttvic, born of the blissful knowledge of the SELF. (37)

That which from the union of the senses with their objects at first is as nectar, but in the end is like venom, that pleasure is accounted râjasic. (38)

That pleasure which both at first and afterwards is delusive of the self, arising from sleep, indolence and heedlessness, that is declared tâmasic. (39)

There is not an entity, either on the earth or again in heaven among the Gods, that is liberated from these three gunas, born of Prakriti. (40)

Of Brâhmans, Kshattriyas, Vaishyas and Shûdras, O Parantapa, the Karmas[1] have been distributed, according to the gunas born of their own natures. (41)

Serenity, self-restraint, austerity, purity, forgiveness and also uprightness, wisdom, knowledge, belief in God, are the Brâhmana-Karma, born of his own nature. (42)

Prowess, splendour, firmness, dexterity, and also not flying from battle, generosity, the nature of a ruler, are the Kshattriya-Karma, born of his own nature. (43)

[1] "Duty" might here be used throughout, but the word Karma is now well understood and is more significant; it is action arising from the nature fashioned by past thoughts and *desires.*

Ploughing, protection of kine, and trade are the Vaisha-Karma, born of his own nature. Action of the nature of service is the Shûdra-Karma, born of his own nature. (44)

Man reacheth perfection by each being intent on his own Karma. Listen thou how perfection is won by him who is intent on his own Karma. (45)

He from whom is the emanation of beings, by Whom all This is pervaded, by worshipping Him in his own Karma a man winneth perfection. (46)

Better is one's own Dharma, though destitute of merits, than the well-executed Dharma of another. He who doeth the Karma laid down by his own nature incurreth not sin. (47)

Nature-born Karma, O son of Kuntî, though defective, ought not to be abandoned. All undertakings indeed are clouded by defects as fire by smoke. (48)

He whose Buddhi is everywhere unattached, the self subdued, dead to desires, he goeth by renunciation to the supreme perfection of freedom from Karma. (49)

How he who hath attained perfection obtaineth Brahman, learn thou from Me only succinctly, O Kaunteya, that highest state of wisdom. (50)

United to Buddhi purified, controlling the self by firmness, having abandoned sound and the other objects of the senses, having laid aside passion and malice, (51)

Dwelling in solitude, abstemious, speech, body and mind[1] subdued, constantly fixed in meditation and Yoga,[2] taking refuge in dispassion, (52)

Having cast aside egoism, violence, arrogance, desire, wrath, covetousness,

[1] Manas.

[2] Some read "dhyânayoga," "Yoga of meditation."

selfless and peaceful—he is fit to become Brahman. (53)

Becoming Brahman, serene in the SELF, he neither grieveth nor desireth; the same to all beings, he obtaineth supreme devotion unto Me. (54)

By devotion he knoweth Me in essence, who and what I am; having thus known Me in essence he forthwith entereth into That. (55)

Though ever performing all actions, taking refuge in Me, by My grace he obtaineth the internal indestructible abode. (56)

Renouncing mentally all works in Me, intent on Me, resorting to Buddhi-Yoga, have thy thought ever on Me. (57)

Thinking on Me, thou shalt overcome all obstacles by My grace; but if from egoism thou wilt not listen, thou shalt be destroyed utterly. (58)

Entrenched in egoism, thou thinkest

"I will not fight;" to no purpose thy determination; nature will constrain thee. (59)

O Son of Kuntî, bound by thine own Karma, born of thine own nature, that which from delusion thou desirest not to do, even that helplessly thou shalt perform. (60)

Îshvara dwelleth in the hearts of all beings, O Arjuna, by His Mâyâ[1] causing all beings to revolve, as though mounted on a potter's wheel. (61)

Flee unto Him for shelter with all thy being, O Bhârata; by His grace thou shalt obtain supreme peace, the everlasting dwelling-place. (62)

Thus hath wisdom, more secret than secrecy (itself), been declared unto thee by Me; having reflected on it fully, then act thou as thou listest. (63)

Listen thou again to My supreme

[1] Illusive power.

word, most secret of all; beloved art thou of Me, and steadfast of heart, therefore will I speak for thy benefit. (64)

Merge thy Manas in Me, be My devotee, sacrifice to Me, prostrate thyself before Me, thou shalt come even to Me. I pledge thee My troth; thou art dear to Me. (65)

Abandoning all Dharmas, come unto Me alone for shelter; sorrow not, I will liberate thee from all sins. (66)

Never is this to be spoken by thee to anyone who is without asceticism, nor without devotion, or as who desireth not to listen, or yet to him who speaketh evil of Me. (67)

He who shall declare this supreme secret among My devotees, having shown the highest devotion for Me, without doubt he shall come to Me.[1] (68)

[1] Some read "asanshaya," which would be "being freed from doubts."

Nor is there any among men who performeth dearer service to Me than he, nor any other than he shall be more beloved by Me on earth. (69)

And he who shall study this sacred dialogue of ours, by him I shall be worshipped with the sacrifice of wisdom. Such is My mind. (70)

The man also who, full of faith, merely heareth it unreviling, even he freed from evil obtaineth the spotless worlds of the righteous. (71)

Has this been heard, O son of Pritha, with one-pointed mind? Has thy delusion, caused by unwisdom, been destroyed O Dhananjaya? (72)

Arjuna said:

Destroyed my delusion. I have gained knowledge [1] through Thy grace, O Achyuta. I am firm, my doubts

[1] Literally "memory."

have fled away. I will do according to Thy word. (73)

Sanjaya said:

I heard this marvellous dialogue of Vâsudeva and of the great soul Pârtha, causing my hair to stand on end; (74)

By the favour of Vyâsa I listened to this secret and supreme Yoga from the Lord of Yoga, Krishna Himself speaking before mine eyes. (75)

O King, remembering, remembering this marvellous and holy dialogue between Keshava and Arjuna, I rejoice again and again. (76)

Remembering, remembering, also that most marvellous form of Hari, great is my wonder, O King. I rejoice, again and again. (77)

Wherever is Krishna, Yoga's Lord, or wherever is Pârtha, the archer, assured are there prosperity, victory and happiness. So I think.[1] (78)

Thus in the glorious Upanishads of the BHAGAVAD GÎTÂ, the science of Brahman, the scripture of Yoga, the dialogue between Shri Krishna and Arjuna, the eighteenth discourse, entitled:

THE YOGA OF LIBERATION BY RENUNCIATION.

Thus the BHAGAVAD GÎTÂ hath ending.

PEACE BE TO ALL WORLDS.

[1] Shri Shânkarâchârya's reading would run, translated: "there is prosperity, victory, happiness, and firm morality."